T0076058

Get the eBook FREE!
(PDF, ePub, Kindle, and liveBook all included)

We believe that once you buy a book from us, you should be able to read it in any format we have available. To get electronic versions of this book at no additional cost to you, purchase and then register this book at the Manning website.

Go to https://www.manning.com/freebook and follow the instructions to complete your pBook registration.

That's it!
Thanks from Manning!

Skills of a Successful Software Engineer

FERNANDO DOGLIO

MANNING
SHELTER ISLAND

For online information and ordering of this and other Manning books, please visit www.manning.com. The publisher offers discounts on this book when ordered in quantity. For more information, please contact

Special Sales Department
Manning Publications Co.
20 Baldwin Road
PO Box 761
Shelter Island, NY 11964
Email: orders@manning.com

Manning Publications Co.
20 Baldwin Road
PO Box 761
Shelter Island, NY 11964

Development editor:	Doug Rudder
Technical development editor:	Rasmus Kirkeby Strøbæk
Review editor:	Mihaela Batinić
Production editor:	Deirdre Hiam
Copy editor:	Andy Carroll
Proofreader:	Katie Tennant
Technical proofreader:	Tim Woolridge
Typesetter:	Gordan Salinovic
Cover designer:	Marija Tudor

ISBN 9781617299704
Printed in the United States of America

To my wife, who's always supported me on every single decision I've made and who's always been by my side on every adventure: this book, just like everything else I do, is thanks to you.

And to my kids, who've mastered the art of making me a proud dad every single day: I love you!

contents

preface

The software development industry has changed, and I'm not talking about a recent change—this happened years ago. Accessing the entry-level knowledge required to start a career in software development is no longer the privilege of a few, but an opportunity for the masses. Knowledge is not the problem—technology has allowed us to make it widespread—but the industry itself hasn't adapted yet.

While most people trying to start a career as a developer focus on the technical side of what to learn (which language and framework to learn, which tutorial is best for understanding design patterns, etc.), they forget about everything else. And through that, they miss out on the most important detail: technical knowledge is readily available, and they will be consuming it for many years, if not decades. In contrast, understanding what to expect from your first job, choosing your first company from several job offers, or even figuring out how to work with a team of colleagues with different levels of skills than yours is not trivial, and that knowledge is less available. There are plenty of aspects of our profession that don't involve coding, and even if they do, they don't rely on code but rather on best practices and teamwork.

That's where this book comes from—the need to fill in that gap in the upbringing of new developers. I strongly believe that anyone can learn how to code if they spend enough time and find the right resources. I honestly believe that is the easiest part of our profession. But the rest? The rest is only learned through experience, and while I can't force experience into you through a book, I can give you a head start by sharing my own. After almost two decades in this industry, I've picked up a tip or two, and I'm more than willing to share them with you.

My hope is that by reading this book you'll either be able to prepare for what's coming, or if you're already getting started, you'll be able to make sense of what you're experiencing. That's all. I'm not going to teach the basics of programming—there is the internet for that (and plenty of other books as well). But if you're interested in knowing what else to expect from the journey you've embarked on, then keep on reading!

acknowledgments

While some people would like to think that a book is the work of a single author, the reality is very different. I'd like to acknowledge everyone who's been involved in the creation of this (and many other titles) within Manning: from the acquisition editor who saw potential in one of my articles on the internet and thought it could become a full-blown book, to the multiple reviewers, editors, and to all the others involved in every single step of the year-long process required to publish the book.

I thank my production editor, Deirdre Hiam; my copyeditor, Andy Carroll; my reviewing editor, Mihaela Batinić; and my proofreader, Katie Tennant. I'd also like to thank the reviewers who took the time to read my manuscript at various stages during its development and who provided invaluable feedback—your suggestions helped make this a better book: Adhir Ramjiawan, Alessandro Puzielli, Brent Boylan, Christopher Villanueva, Deepak Raghavan, Dze Richard Fang, Fabian Pietro de Franca Bram, Jeremy Chen, Jessica Daubner, João Marcelo Borovina Josko, Joseph Pereniaj, Krzysztof Hrynczenko, Lobel Strmečki, Matthias Busch, Mattia Antonino Di Gangi, Mikael Dautrey, Oliver Korten, Owain Williams, Rodney Weis, Samantha Berk, Samvid Mistry, Simone Sguazza, Stuart Ellis, Sveta Ashokchandra Natu, and Tim Wooldridge.

about this book

Skills of a Successful Software Engineer was written with the aim of helping newcomers to the industry by sharing my own experience, my own mistakes, and the lessons I've learned from them. It's intended to give you a glimpse into your future and to show you a possible pathway to traverse it. In the end, the way you evolve and move forward is going to be your own.

Who should read this book

Everyone!

At least, that's my hope, but on a more serious note, I've written this book for a very specific type of reader: someone who's just getting started and has potentially not even worked as a developer yet. That person will get the most out of this book.

However, through our review process, we've also discovered that many developers with years-long careers already under their belts were able to learn a thing or two from different chapters. Some of them had been working for the same company all this time, and they found chapter 6 about the interview process interesting. Others have been toying around with the idea of working on a side project but didn't know where to begin, so chapter 5 was great for them. There is something for everyone here, so I encourage you to take a look, even if you've been working for a while already.

How this book is organized

It wasn't easy, but I tried to organize the content of this book into a logical progression. The eight chapters try to parallel the evolution of your career as a developer:

- Chapter 1 covers the basis of a software development career: what should be your focus and what are some of the biggest misconceptions people have about the industry. If you're still on the fence about whether this is the right career choice for you, this chapter should help you answer that question.

- Chapter 2 will walk you through some of the core concepts you'll need to understand when tackling code. No, they're not code-related concepts; I'm not talking about `if` statements or `for` loops. This chapter covers ideas such as understanding that there is no perfect code, and that you need to document your logic even if you're the only one working on it. There are many ways to go about writing code, and this chapter will show you some best practices to keep you sane while doing it.

- Chapter 3 is the first technical chapter of the book, and it covers unit testing. The concepts covered here are valid for any language you might decide to work with. The few code samples here are either in JavaScript or Python, but they'll feel more like pseudocode than anything. The point of this chapter is not for you to copy and paste code and get it running, but rather to help you understand why unit testing is such a crucial task and to present the core concepts around it.

- Chapter 4 is the last technical chapter of the book, and it covers another core practice within our industry: refactoring. Again, the focus of this chapter is not the code; instead, it discusses why refactoring is such an integral part of our career and best methods for tackling it.

- Chapter 5 tackles the personal side of coding, with advice on how to balance your need to code and learn against the fact that you also have a life outside of your computer. Burnout is real in our industry, and sometimes it results from the need to keep on learning, so in this chapter I cover some aspects of what that means and how to move forward without burning out.

- Chapter 6 focuses on the technical interview process. This can be a very stressful process for some, and very scary for others. I've gone through plenty of interviews (on both sides) during my career, and here I share some insights into how to best prepare for them as well as to what to expect from the process.

- Chapter 7 assumes you've started working for a company and that you're part of a team. In this chapter, I cover team dynamics, understanding what your manager expects from you, controlling your developer ego, and more. The way you code is influenced by these dynamics, so don't disregard the importance of this chapter!

- Chapter 8 finishes the book with an overview of what it means to be a leader. Why? Because it's the natural progression of most developers: you start as a junior developer and eventually are presented with the opportunity to lead a small team. You might like it or you might hate it—they're both very valid outcomes. However, often people forget to tell you what it means to actually lead a team, and this chapter tries to present some insights into that role.

From understanding what it means to be a developer to getting some insight into what it will mean to lead your first team, this book covers a wide range of topics. This is my view of the process, and you don't need to follow every piece of advice or perform every action the same way I suggest. However, by getting a glimpse into what's awaiting you and some analysis of the different options, you'll be able to make the best decisions for your own context and desires.

About the code

The focus of this book is not on the code. The little snippets you'll see, especially in chapters 3 and 4, are written in either JavaScript, Python, or plain pseudocode. By themselves, the snippets will not likely work or produce any meaningful results, so don't focus on getting them to run. They're there to illustrate the concepts I'm discussing, so just consider them in conjunction with the explanation I give in those sections.

liveBook discussion forum

Purchase of *Skills of a Successful Software Engineer* includes free access to liveBook, Manning's online reading platform. Using liveBook's exclusive discussion features, you can attach comments to the book globally or to specific sections or paragraphs. It's a snap to make notes for yourself, ask and answer technical questions, and receive help from the author and other users. To access the forum, go to https://livebook .manning.com/book/skills-of-a-successful-software-engineer/discussion. You can also learn more about Manning's forums and the rules of conduct at https://livebook .manning.com/discussion.

Manning's commitment to our readers is to provide a venue where a meaningful dialogue between individual readers and between readers and the author can take place. It is not a commitment to any specific amount of participation on the part of the author, whose contribution to the forum remains voluntary (and unpaid). We suggest you try asking the author some challenging questions lest his interest stray! The forum and the archives of previous discussions will be accessible from the publisher's website as long as the book is in print.

about the author

 **FERNANDO DOGLIO** has been working in the software industry for the past 19 years. He started building websites and working with Java-Script, HTML, and CSS in 2003. Between then and now, Fernando experienced some of the most popular web technologies, such as Ruby, Python, PHP, and Node.js (working with several of its frameworks and creating a set of custom ones as well).

He made the jump from web to big data, using his experience with microservices and incorporating the use of big data–related solutions (such as Kafka, Hadoop, NoSQL databases, Spark, and the like) to become a senior architect developing and creating cloud solutions that were both highly available and fault tolerant.

He then started transitioning into a leading role, where he dealt with the technical difficulties of different teams, as well as being the technical point of contact for clients.

Finally, during the last six years of his career, Fernando has been working as a technical manager, leading multiple high-end projects and overseeing different aspects of the day-to-day work of developers.

about the cover illustration

The figure on the cover of *Skills of a Successful Software Engineer* is "Femme de Barabinze," or "Woman from Barabinze," taken from a collection by Jacques Grasset de Saint-Sauveur, published in 1797. Each illustration is finely drawn and colored by hand.

In those days, it was easy to identify where people lived and what their trade or station in life was just by their dress. Manning celebrates the inventiveness and initiative of the computer business with book covers based on the rich diversity of regional culture centuries ago, brought back to life by pictures from collections such as this one.

Becoming a successful software engineer

1

This chapter covers

- Avoiding misconceptions about initial skill requirements
- Focusing on skills that will help you become a better software developer

From the outside, the software industry looks very compelling: many countries have no unemployment in the industry, salaries are fair, there is always room to grow, travel is often involved, and there is the option to work from your couch for a Silicon Valley startup. Why isn't everyone working on software?

The truth is that while the field might seem interesting, getting in is not that simple. I knew I wanted to be a software developer before I owned my first computer. I made the choice when I was a kid, based on the value computers were generating even then. But when it was time for me to jump into the real world, it wasn't just difficult to get in, it was scary and unwelcoming. I had no guide, no map that would help me navigate the maze that was job interviews or even job listings. I would spend a few hours every weekend going through the Jobs section of my local newspaper, looking for opportunities for junior developers without experience.

Finding your first job as a software developer can be challenging at best; most companies looking for entry-level engineers require them to either have experience with some of the latest frameworks and technologies or to understand a lot of advanced concepts such as design patterns, software development best practices, and version control. Then they'll go into vague requirements, such as having great "interpersonal skills" or knowledge about other IT-related areas. What is that about?

I compiled the following junior developer job listing from multiple samples on the internet:

- Bachelor's degree in related areas and a minimum of one year of experience in similar roles
- Knowledge of secure software development
- Intermediate skills associated with design, development, modifications, and deployment of software, including object-oriented programming
- Knowledge of other IT-related areas
- Proof of software repository skills
- Proof of effective communication and interpersonal skills
- Self-motivated and works independently
- Proof of problem-solving skills
- Intermediate skills in C#, ASP.NET MVC, SQL Server, TypeScript, and React.js
- Experience using Git and GitHub

Looking at that list, how can anyone trying to get into the industry not feel intimidated? Anyone looking at that job posting will assume they need at least two more years of experience before being taken seriously.

Having been through the same experience 18 years ago, I still remember the type of questions I had:

- Should I even bother applying for the job? I only have 3 of the 10 required skills.
- Do I need to stop studying *X* and switch to *Y* now? This week everyone's asking for *Y* developers.
- How can I get experience if I'm looking for my first job?

They're probably the same questions that any new developer looking to start their career has. But here's the kicker: these questions are normal. You're not figuring out that you're not cut out to be a developer—you're just living through the junior developer experience.

That's why I'm writing this book: to help you find your way into a successful career. I've been through the same struggles that any new developer experiences, and I've had an underpaid first job because I had no experience. I've met some great people who through me quite a lot about working in a team, and I've met some difficult people who, through their behavior, taught me a considerable amount about what to avoid.

Throughout this book, I'll be sharing bits and pieces of my own journey. I'll cover the best practices you'll have to apply to your code, and I'll take you through some core technical concepts such as unit testing and refactoring so you understand what they mean and the importance they have in a software project. I'll help you understand how to balance your personal and professional life without burning out in the process, and I'll give you some hints for your first technical interview. In the end, I'll go into what it means to be a developer working inside a bigger team, and I'll discuss what it means to lead a team, so you understand what your manager is going through with you. Throughout this book I hope to show you that you're just getting started in your journey, and that the issues you're facing and the doubts you're having are completely normal. They're part of the developer-experience pack you bought when you decided to live off your coding skills.

In this chapter, I'll start by covering the basics: what exactly do you need in order to work as a developer? There is a lot of noise on the internet, and asking this question on Google can bring up a lot of different articles. Everyone has their opinion, and most people tend to focus on functional skills—the things you need to learn before thinking of applying for a job. In my experience, they're not the most relevant skills, nor the most important ones. You'll pick those up through experience if you have to. The truly important qualities of a good developer (even one who's never worked a single day in their life) are not technical.

We'll look at two lists in this chapter: the common misconceptions of what you need to be a developer, and the truly useful skills you'll actually need.

1.1 What you don't need

I'll start by covering some of the biggest misconceptions around the requirements for getting into the software industry. None of the following qualifications will hurt your chances, but they're not hard requirements needed to start the job. Don't think of this as a to-do list, but rather, a nice-to-eventually-have list.

1.1.1 Bachelor's degree in CS or related degree

This is essentially four or more years of formal education. I went through it, I did my best to finish it, and I failed on my first try. I tried to be a "Software Engineer," a five-year course of study in my country, but by the time I was halfway through my studies I got my first job, and my formal education ended there.

Did I regret it? I did, which is why a few years later I completed a technical degree (two years plus a final project) to formalize a lot of my practical experience. Did I need the first two years of university? I did, yes, but mainly because they formalized a lot of the basic programming concepts I had figured out on my own, learning how to code for fun. But back then there were no bootcamps, my internet access was limited by my 2,400 baud modem, and my learning resources were mainly hacker e-magazines (which were text files with some ASCII art thrown in).

The situation now is completely different; anyone looking to learn how to code has the world's knowledge at their disposal. This is no exaggeration; there are free online resources such as YouTube or freeCodeCamp (www.freeCodeCamp.org), which have everything you need to go from zero to workable. And while it is true that not everyone can learn on their own, you also have other options: paid courses from sites like Udemy or Skillshare, which will cost a lot less than a university degree and will give you access to virtual classrooms, Q&A sessions with teachers, and contact with other students going through the same problems you are.

Any of these resources can give you the practical knowledge required to start coding, and while it is true that many people value the mention of a college degree as part of your resume, a lot of companies are paying less attention to that single bullet point. Granted, this may be less true in some countries than others, but it's also true that ours is a very international profession in the sense that we can work for companies anywhere in the world. When that starts happening, the value of a college degree starts diminishing as time goes by. I've personally performed hundreds of interviews with new developers, and I've learned that a college degree should not be an entry requirement.

Don't get me wrong. I believe there is still value in formal education, and I'll go into more detail about that later on, but it's not necessarily your best choice if you're looking to get your first developer job. Especially if you're in a hurry, a 4-or-more-year investment (money *and* time) may well be too much; when compared to 6 to 12 months for a practical bootcamp, the choice should be obvious.

Do you need more? Yes, of course. A bootcamp or online education won't cover everything you need to know, but that's not what we're after here. We're focusing on the practical aspects of the profession, so you can start learning by doing.

1.1.2   *Knowing the software development lifecycle*

A typical software project has to go through a development lifecycle:

1 You first need to do a requirement analysis to understand exactly what you need to do.
2 You then move on to planning your project to understand when you'll need to do those things and how much time you'll need.
3 Designing the project architecture comes third. Once you know the "what" and the "when," you have to start thinking about the "how," and the architecture will give you the blueprints for that.
4 Only then can you start writing code. This is the step that most developers tend to focus on, but as you can see, it's not the first thing you'd normally do.
5 Testing your code and your product comes next. Determining whether the previous step produced the right output is a must-do before moving on to the next one.
6 Deploying your product is the final step. This is when you give it to users so they can start testing it and giving you feedback.

Because it's a cycle, you'd take that feedback from step 6 and start all over again, but you get the idea.

If you've never worked on a software project before, you've never had to apply most of these concepts, and that's perfectly fine. You don't need to understand any of that to get your first job. Yes, these steps will be part of your tasks, and you'll be applying this knowledge every day. But turning it into an entry-level requirement for the role of junior developer is like asking an acting surgeon to lead their first surgery. Eventually they'll be able to do that, and they've probably read about it, but you don't want them doing it on day one. It's the same for you as a developer. You should not be expected to understand what all these steps really mean on day one—you won't be in charge of doing it anyway. You'll learn about it because you'll be part of the process.

1.1.3 *A math, physics, or similar degree*

I'm guilty of believing this one myself, back when I started. I blame college because they were teaching me calculus and algebra at the same time I was learning to code. Was that a mistake? In the long run, no, but it did nothing to help me get my first job as a developer.

Math, physics, or other sciences are not going to help you understand programming. Some of them require you to understand abstract concepts (such as infinity, or the number pi), which can be good practice when you need to create mental models of an algorithm you're trying to write. However, you won't be solving hard math problems or implementing difficult physics simulations on your first job, and even if you happen to find yourself in such a conundrum, there is a big chance you'll be using someone else's code library.

So should you get a math degree before making the jump to computer science or a junior developer role? No, not at all. Eventually you might find shared concepts between programming and these other sciences (such as sets in many programming languages), or you might find yourself implementing concepts from other realms in your code (such as implementing the concept of gravity on a platform game), but none of this requires a full degree before starting to code.

> **NOTE** The role of a junior data scientist might require you to have a math or science degree. That requirement is not for understanding how to code but rather how to model the problems you're trying to solve.

1.1.4 *Certifications*

Certifications are tempting because they have that "not-as-long-as-formal-education-but-still-useful" kind of vibe. And they do have their merit, but they're not a hard requirement to get a developer job.

Listing certifications on your junior developer resume shows you care about your learning and about improving your skills. This is indeed a good thing, but it's not a requirement. You won't find job listings for a junior developer asking for particular certifications. Instead, they'll be looking for knowledge about a group of technologies, and this is easier to achieve by following online courses or bootcamps.

What I'm saying here is, if you have to choose between investing in a certification or an online course, go for the latter. Get a broader education before you start narrowing down on a particular subject.

1.1.5   *The desire to work in a fast-paced environment*

You can find this requirement in many job listings and in basic software development skill sets. But what does "fast-paced" even mean here? It could mean almost anything, but I'm assuming (because that is what anyone reading a job listing would do) it means you have to be interested in working in an industry that changes a lot. And by that, I mean the technologies, working methodologies, project focus, or even projects themselves change.

That probably sounds scary, especially for someone who's not even working yet. But I can confirm that you can be a software developer and still hate "fast-paced" environments. Not everyone likes changing technologies, or even changing projects. You don't have to, either.

Granted, startups normally work that way because they have to. They normally need to grow fast and adapt to changes. Contractors work like that too. There are companies out there that will hire you to be part of someone's team for the duration of a project, and when that's done, you move on to the next client. If you find those scenarios interesting, go ahead and apply. Chances are you'll enjoy your work there.

But there are other companies—ones that have been working for years on their products—that tend to have a more stable environment. In fact, the perfect example of that is banks (I should know; I've worked for some of them as an external contractor). They have so much data from so many clients that making a change to their tech stack is quite hard and, honestly, scary for them.

There is no right choice here. Most of the time you don't get to choose your first company—the fact that they accept your lack of experience will be the deciding factor. However, keep in mind that just because a section of our industry is "fast-paced" doesn't mean *you* need to like it or to be looking for that.

1.1.6   *Experience*

Asking for experience from a junior developer is not only counterintuitive, it's just plain silly. And I've been there. I know how it feels when you read a job listing asking for junior developers with experience in different technologies. You're reading the listing trying to find a job so you can get the experience. It's the egg and chicken problem.

My advice is to ignore that part of the listing. It makes no sense, after all. Apply if you feel comfortable with some of the other requirements or if you feel like you can pick them up quickly.

If you're applying for the job and are worried about the experience part, you can showcase the types of experience you do have:

- If you've done some kind of online course, you can list it here.
- If you have published one or more personal projects somewhere (on GitHub, or somewhere else), you will definitely want to list it here.
- If you've worked as a volunteer on something remotely related to IT, list it here.

Requiring experience for an entry-level position makes no sense, so listing experience should not be a prerequisite. But if you do want to address that point on your application, listing some of the preceding items is definitely better than saying "none."

1.2 Useful skills to have

On the other end of the spectrum are skills that are never listed in typical job offers but that will help you to get your first job or to be considered a great developer. They're not technical skills, though, so many new developers tend to omit them from their resumes.

These are passive skills. You won't actively have to use them; rather, they'll be there in the back of your mind helping you in your daily routine. The most frustrating part about these skills is that there are no online courses or bootcamps that will help you train. These are soft skills that you need to be aware of in order to develop them (if you don't already have them).

I know that's probably not what you wanted to hear, but these skills are the cornerstone of growing as a developer. Any technical skill can be learned over time by reading a manual or watching a video. But the skills discussed in this section will be there, helping you through that learning process. Yes, you'll become a developer by learning how to code, but if you skip these five skills, it'll be like learning to run before knowing how to walk.

1.2.1 Patience

Nothing says "I'm a software developer" like spending three hours debugging a piece of code, just to figure out that the problem was a missing comma somewhere in the middle. You'll go through this *a lot*, and that is no sign of "juniority" or of lack of experience. Trust me, I go through that same process every now and then today, after almost 20 years.

Understanding someone else's code requires time and effort; researching how to solve a problem requires time and effort; writing code and getting it to work requires time and effort. Patience is not a virtue for a developer, it's a must-have. Copying and pasting code from the internet will only get you half way. The rest needs to come from you, and there is a lot of trial and error involved.

1.2.2 Determination

In line with patience is determination—you have to understand that this is not an easy profession. I'm not saying this to scare you off. On the contrary, setting the right expectations is key to avoiding discouragement when bad things happen during your journey.

The fact is that your chosen profession will be filled with roadblocks, with problems that once fixed become ten. You will encounter bugs that take months to solve, and each and every one of these situations will become a reason for you to quit. Trust me, I've wanted to quit programming multiple times during my career. The idea of moving to the middle of nowhere, away from technology, and growing tomatoes in the desert is appealing to many developers in our industry. Is that the sign of a problem in software development? I don't think so, but it is proof that ours can be a frustrating profession at times.

That is why determination is a must-have skill for developers, and you can build it up over time. It's hard to know if you're determined enough until you're faced with a situation that challenges you, but if you're already a determined person—someone who's known to not give up on the first try—you'll do fine as a developer.

1.2.3 *An eternal student mindset*

The underlying topic of this book is professional growth; you might have picked that up from browsing the table of contents. However, growth can't happen without learning. I'll cover learning in chapter 5, but I still want to highlight it here.

One hard requirement I would demand from every new software developer is that they should always be learning, or at least be open to the idea of learning. While it is true that you don't have to like a fast-paced work environment, our industry is always moving. Sometimes it moves forward, and sometimes it goes backward, making a 20-year-old pattern new again (I'm looking at you, React), and if you don't keep tabs on these changes, you'll be left behind.

I'm not saying you need to go out and learn "all the things." What I'm saying is that you should be open to the idea that the tools you're using right now and the things you know right now will not always be the norm. If you don't accept that, you'll find yourself unable to move forward in your career within two years.

Technology pushes technology forward; it's that simple. The tools you use today will not be the same as the ones you'll use tomorrow. New technology developments will open new areas of research, new ways of processing data, and new ways of interacting with users, and when that happens, development tools will have to adapt. If you don't adapt with them, you'll be left behind.

1.2.4 *Accepting criticism and learning from it*

Programming is not a solo profession. Even if you're considering going freelance, you'll have to interact with other developers in one way or another. And part of that interaction happens through feedback.

Code review, for example, is a very common practice in software development. It ensures code quality by having a group of developers review the code written by someone else. If you've never been through it, it might sound strange, but it can be a growing experience for both parties if they perform it correctly:

- On the reviewing end, the group of developers reading the code need to understand that their job is to improve the code by finding logic issues, missing standards, or even some bugs.
- On the receiving end, you'll need to understand that the feedback they're giving you is not personal. Displaying your code for this kind of review can feel like that nightmare where you realize a little too late that you're already in class, naked, in front of everyone. But trust me, the reviewers are putting their years of experience at your disposal. Accept their feedback, make sure you understand why it is given, and you'll come out learning a lot.

There are other instances where feedback will come into play as well. Sometimes you'll be expecting it, like with performance reviews, and other times you won't, like when an issue is reported on your open source project. Surviving negative feedback, especially when it's not expected, can be hard if you're not open to learning from it.

I think it's important to distinguish between feedback that shows a negative quality in our work (such as identifying a bug) and nonconstructive (negative) feedback that only shows how our work has affected others, to the point where they need to hurt or disqualify us with their words. There is always a nugget of wisdom in negative feedback; you just have to ignore the negative coating around it, and cut through to the core message and the lesson to be taken from it. You should consider the rest to be noise.

As a technical lead, I've received hundreds of performance reviews in my career, and they've not always been positive. Whenever that happens, I always try to focus on getting to the core of the problem, to what caused that negative review so that I can avoid that behavior in the future.

If you only see feedback as a bad thing, you'll start second-guessing your decisions, and the whole point of that feedback (which was to help you improve) will be lost.

1.2.5 *Knowing how to communicate*

This is a tough one, because a very common problem among developers, even experienced ones, is that they don't know how to communicate well with people. Sometimes we focus so much on learning how to write logic code for machines that our soft skills, no matter how small and undeveloped they are, tend to wither away. Machines don't need us to write eloquent sentences, and they don't really care for synonyms or the use of metaphors and figurative speech. They need clear, unquestionable logic. However, as a developer, you also need to work with humans, who, unlike machines, favor all those things.

When you need to ask a colleague for help and explain a problem you're having, or when you have to solve someone else's problem, you'll need to switch from your "machine-understandable syntax" to your "human-understandable" settings. This is why having communication skills before applying to your first job will give you a major advantage over everyone else in your situation. The moment your interviewer notices you can communicate effectively, the battle is half won.

How can you develop this skill? One way to do it is through writing. Back when I started, both my written and spoken communication skills were terrible. I remember spending 30 minutes writing "important" emails because I had to go through them multiple times, adding words and explanations and asking colleagues to review them to see if they made sense or not.

It was only when I started making a conscious effort to write online (articles for my own blog) that I started learning how to write more eloquently. You can say I started finding human-friendly ways of explaining concepts. This, in turn, helped my spoken communication skills as well—something "clicked" in my brain. Through that and other working experiences, I was able to learn how to effectively talk to others, which then helped me in my path to leading teams as well.

Knowing how to communicate well with others is an important skill to have, and the great news is that you can start practicing it right now, for free.

1.3 What about after you get the job?

The trick to having a successful career as a software developer is to remember that you're not done when you get your job. You're just getting started. Getting the job is like getting to the max level on your favorite MMORPG and thinking you beat the game, when, in fact, you just unlocked a whole new level of content specifically designed for you. Getting the job doesn't mean you've mastered the trade; it just means you're now standing on the first step of a huge ladder. The skills I listed in this chapter will have to be developed and maintained throughout the course of your life, and the more you work on them, the better you'll do.

The rest of this book will cover other areas you'll need to focus on once you've decided to become a software developer, and they are just as important as the ones covered here. But always keep these skills in mind, as they'll be the building blocks for everything else you learn in the coming chapters.

Summary

- Keep honing your communication skills. They'll always be useful, but the higher on the ladder you climb, the more important they'll become.
- Understanding how to grow from negative feedback will keep you from getting stuck in your career.
- Working on your patience and determination will ensure you never meet a problem you can't solve. These two skills have taught me that nothing is impossible in our profession, as long as you have enough time and people to work on it.
- Staying relevant in our industry is a must for anyone who's interested in advancing their career. That means looking outside your own box (outside your daily work) to find out what others are doing. Technology evolves constantly, so keep an eye on it.

Writing code
everyone can read

This chapter covers

- Focusing on working code first
- Writing code that's understandable to the whole team
- Ways around overengineering
- Eliminating apparently random bugs
- Learning about languages you don't normally use

During your journey as a developer, one of the main activities in your day is going to be coding. Writing code needs to become part of your life, not because you want to make a living out of it, but because you're looking to be great at it. Just as any Olympic athlete spends a portion of their day training and the rest of it thinking about their training, you need to do the same. If you're aiming to become an Olympic coder (granted, that's not a thing, but it should be) you need to make code your life.

I'm not asking you to forfeit time with your loved ones, but keeping code in the back of your mind is something that you'll want to do. While that might sound a bit vague, my point is that the intrinsic logic behind the act of coding—what's usually known as Boolean logic—should be present in all you do. That's how, when you sit down to write some code, the logic will just flow out of your fingers.

You will never improve by repeating a task if you just keep mindlessly doing it over and over again. You need to understand what to aim for. Be clear about the standards you have to achieve and the best practices to follow. Only then will you be able to measure your progress and understand whether you're improving. That's what I mean by "keeping code in the back of your mind." You'll be solving problems and thinking about algorithms even without noticing.

This book is not going to teach you how to code; you should already know how to do that. What I *will* cover are some of the lessons I've learned about the process of coding.

If you've been coding for a while, you might recognize some of the behaviors and problems I'll mention in this chapter. If you're just starting on your coding journey, you might consider some of them obvious or trivial right now, but take them to heart, because you'll soon start seeing how easy it is to fall for these traps.

You could say that this will be an *inception* chapter. I'll be presenting lots of ideas that you may not usually think about, but once they get in the back of your mind, they'll become a major guiding force for your coding decisions in the future.

2.1   *Your code needs to work*

The first concept I want to get into your head is that your code needs to work. This might sound obvious, but bear with me. When you're writing code, the first version you write only needs to have a single purpose: to do whatever job you need it to do. The initial goal is not to solve the problem quickly, or to solve it using the least amount of resources, or to fit any other constraints you might come up with. Your code just needs to work.

Imagine being assigned the task of delivering a working prototype for a new system sign-up form in under a week. A prototype is just a simpler version of the final product—something that helps you see how it will work but that you know will require more work before releasing it into production. You and your team know that a completely functional feature like this requires two months of work. You'll need to consider things like where the user directory will be stored, the auth methods you'll allow and how they're integrated, whether you'll let users sign in through their Google account or GitHub, how their APIs work, and so on. There are many questions to answer before you can call it done. In this case, though, we're just thinking about a simple prototype, probably using a MySQL database to store passwords as plain text. Nobody cares about that part right now; they just want to see it working.

The question then is how you would tackle your part of the code. You have at least a couple of options. If you think you know where the feature is going in the future, you can create placeholder entities and maybe even code some methods, trying to do some work ahead of time. This approach assumes that you'll be using this code as is in the next iteration of the feature. That sounds smart, right? Work now, so you don't have to work later. Or as others would put it, *don't leave for tomorrow what you can do today*. Alternatively, you can simply code the bare minimum to make it work, since you expect most of the feature will be reworked for its next version, given how many things in the backend will change.

How would you tackle it? Would you go the extra mile and pave the way for the next version? Or would you write some throwaway code that will only prove your point right now?

2.1.1 *Good is better than perfect*

Thinking we can create a perfect piece of code, especially on our first try, is not only foolish but misguided. It's also a perfectly understandable trap to fall for if you're just starting out, so don't let my harsh words get to you.

Perfection is in the eye of the beholder, and that is true even for code. We as developers tend to consider our code a work of art, and like every artist, we get attached to our creations. Yet, as Stephen King says in his book *On Writing*, "Kill your darlings, kill your darlings, even when it breaks your egocentric little scribbler's heart." Why am I quoting the master of horror in my book aimed at developers? Because he says authors should understand that every line in their book needs to fulfill a purpose in the story. No matter how great a sentence might sound or how intriguing a plot might be, if it doesn't add value to the story, then it doesn't belong there. It's a way of saying that you have to edit yourself.

As a developer, your lines of code are your darlings, and you shouldn't be afraid to kill them. You have to think about the end goal of the logic you're writing. Are you and the rest of your team trying to pave the way to the next version, or are you thinking ahead and spending extra time working on something that will be redone entirely in the next sprint? There is a time and a place to create beautiful code, and the first iteration of a new feature is usually not it. There is nothing wrong with code that just works.

You have to consider the context of your tasks before you decide what approach you'll take when working on them:

- Are you working on a first workable version of something? If so, your best bet is to focus on functionality, not on lines of code, or how modular or SOLID (more on this in a bit) your code is.
- Will your work be used in production, or will it be shared as a library with other teams? If so, yes, worry about making it work *and* keeping it clean.

Remember, you're not writing code for yourself; you're writing code for someone who's expecting it and who has created a timeline based on how quickly your team can deliver the work. If you decide to do some unrequested extra work, you're essentially decreasing the speed of your team and affecting someone else's timeline. Remember that little piece of extra work you thought was helping? It didn't really help anyone.

2.1.2   Working, then optimized

What if instead of paving the way ahead and focusing on features not needed right now, you want to make sure your code runs as fast as possible, or uses as little memory or as few cycles as possible? The question here is, did anybody ask for the code to work under these constraints? Let's go back to the "work of art" thing. You're not painting the next Sistine Chapel, so unless someone requests that you paint a lot of butt naked people reaching for each other on the ceiling, stick to what you have to do. In short, don't fall for the early optimization trap.

We've all been there: starting to optimize our code even before we run it once is a real temptation. The problem is that to optimize something, you first need to be able to measure its performance. Guessing what that performance will look like won't cut it. You have to have numbers before and after your optimizations to compare the results. Without that data, how could we think that optimizing code during development makes any sense?

But why is early optimization a bad idea? It's mainly because without numbers to base your optimizations on, you're making assumptions about the environment you'll be working in and the requirements for your code (how fast it has to run, or how few resources it needs to use). Assumptions like these usually turn into restrictions, which can cause problems.

For example, maybe you're thinking that your code needs to run in under 100 milliseconds, but you have a `for` loop iterating over a list of URLs and making a request for each one. It's impossible for you to make the 100 millisecond mark, so instead you may assume you can cache the content of those URL requests. That's a great assumption, unless you end up needing the real-time rather than cached values.

See what happened there? Following the assumption about how quickly the code needs to run would have you adding extra logic to implement caching, and that caching would never be used if the data needs to be refreshed every time you make the requests. You probably read the word "cache" and immediately thought it was a great solution. However, you kept reading and realized the extra context made a big difference.

To avoid falling for the early optimization trap, don't worry about optimization and focus on understanding the context. Worry about getting the first version of your code doing what it is meant to do. Only then, once you understand how all the pieces fit together, should start thinking about optimizing it (after properly measuring its performance, of course).

2.1.3   Sometimes terrible code actually helps

I'm going to keep saying this throughout the book: writing code is like creating a work of art. It might not seem like that at first, but with time you'll start seeing the art within the lines. You'll start noticing how you can put your personal touch into a piece of code. That's why we all want to make our code look the best it can. You would never try to sell an unfinished song or a half-finished painting. Your code similarly needs to be spot on before you call it "done" (which does not mean being perfect by any means—we already covered that).

However, getting your code to the point where it's "done" is not the same as writing it for the first time. The first version of your solution doesn't have to be pretty. In fact, it can, and sometimes should, be as ugly as possible and smell just as bad. You should think about the first version of your code as the written-down version of the mental model you use to solve the problem. As with any good mental model, it will be high-level and generic, so your first code version will not yield the best result. But that's fine—you should think about it as an initial form in clay. It's not shaped correctly yet, and it doesn't look quite right, but with some effort you can get it to look the way you want. Code can be clay—it can take time to get it right, and trying to do so on your first go will only cause you to fall for one of the traps covered in this chapter (such as early optimization or overengineering).

My advice for any new developer starting to get their hands dirty with code is to embrace the terrible solution and the code smells. They will give you a working version (which already is a win in my book) that you can then sculpt into its final form. And to clarify, *code smells* are essentially bad practices that we use while writing our code and eventually need to remove. We will go over them in chapter 4, but you should know that while they're bad and will have to be removed as much as possible from the final version of your code, you are allowed to use them during your first versions. At this point, the only one reading and maintaining your code is you, so you won't be affected by those smells, at least for the time being.

Code smells are not the only problem you're allowed to introduce in your first solution:

- Nested loops? Sure, add as many and as nested as you need right now.
- Recursion? Sure, why not? Who's going to care about the stack at this point?
- Are you duplicating code all over the place? Fantastic!

See the pattern? These are things you don't want in your final version, if you can avoid them; they'll cause performance issues and memory problems, and they'll make your code hard to maintain. However, you're getting the work done—this ugly, terrible version of your code solves your problem. You won. You've solved the puzzle.

Once that's done, you're allowed (and honestly, highly encouraged) to make it look better. At that point, you can start optimizing and removing those problematic sections. That's when you focus on the people reading your code and forget about the machines for a while. Clean it up, as they say.

2.2 Code for people, not for the machine

When you write code, you shouldn't be thinking about the interpreter or the compiler or how it'll be translated into machine code. That's not your concern. Instead, you should be focusing on who's going to read it tomorrow. Even if you think no one else will read it but you, your focus should still be the same. You see, coding sometimes requires us to come up with intricate solutions, and they won't always make sense the next day, even if you're the one who wrote them. So even if you're alone with your code, write it for you, not for the machine it needs to run on.

Let's continue with the example from the previous section. Let's pretend your new feature works so well that you and your team are now faced with the task of implementing a full version. You and three of your teammates will be writing code for the same feature, which will require people to interact with each other and to write on each other's files. That's completely normal and expected. However, only two days after you start working on it, your team is having daily meetings to review each other's work and understand how the logic works. You're all spending a lot of time understanding code instead of writing it.

Your tech lead asks all of you for an alternative solution to your meetings. What can you do to solve this problem now and for the rest of the project's duration? What would be your suggestion?

2.2.1 *Self-documenting code is a lie*

One terrible solution some developers suggest to solve this problem is to write code that avoids complex logic, using very mnemotechnic variable and function names (such as `monthly_revenue` and `current_index` instead of `foo` and `bar`). Essentially, they say the code will be so clean and easy to read that it will, itself, be the documentation. Clear code is indeed a very good practice and something you should aim for, but it's not enough. It may well work until deadlines hit or the weekend comes and you want to go home—then `user_with_too_many_logins` becomes `foo`, and the whole self-documenting plan goes away.

Whatever solution you come up with needs to scale with code density, and it needs to keep working over long periods of time. Saying you'll document it *eventually* won't work, because documenting two months' worth of code is a massive task. A solution that takes more time than writing the actual code won't work either. You have to find a balance between the two.

I'll show you a few options, and you can pick the one that works best for you and your context. Keep in mind that the goal is to reduce the cognitive load of the person reading your code. The code is designed to be parsed into machine code, so it has a particular structure, but people don't parse and think the same way machines do. We're slower, and our memory is faulty, so we tend to get lost in the logic when reading large chunks of code—we forget where a piece of data is coming from. Whatever solution you implement should help in that regard.

COMMENTING YOUR CODE

Adding comments to your code is the most obvious option. All commonly used programming languages support comments. However, you can't be satisfied with just writing comments—they need to make sense, be useful, and be kept up to date. Take a look at the great comment line in the following listing.

Listing 2.1 Sample `log-in` function for our fictional `log-in` form

```
//log-in function
async function performLogin(username, password, database) {
    let user = await database.query("select * from users where " +
    "usr_name ='" + username + "' and password = '" + password + "'")
    if(!user) {
        return null
    }
    user.last_login = new Date()
    await user.save()
    return user
}
```

This could be a piece of logic for the new sign-up feature you're working on. It's not very clean, and it uses a simplistic approach, but just look at that useful comment at the top. After reading it, do you understand how to use the function, or what the function is meant to do? That comment literally serves no purpose, and I've seen comments like that countless times (heck, I wrote comments like that back in the day too).

For a comment to be useful and provide real help in diminishing the reader's cognitive load, it needs to do the following:

- *Add value to the reader*—What is value in this case? Anything the reader can't know by looking at the function's signature, or by looking at the line of code that the comment is meant to explain. A comment for a block of code should explain the internal logic and mention the steps involved in the process. It can also include information you couldn't possibly have otherwise, such as the types of variables in JavaScript code. A comment on a function or a method that returns something should mention the returned value. What type is it? Comments should explain anything and everything someone else trying to use your code might need to know. Otherwise, readers are back to asking people or making mistakes.
- *Be up to date*—Hoping an outdated comment will help you figure out the code is as realistic as looking at the night sky and thinking the stars still look like that right now. Any of them could have gone supernova already, and you won't find out for thousands of years. The same goes for the comments. If they're not updated when the code is, you're reading an explanation of an older version of the code, which really only adds confusion and bugs to the mix. If you're updating code, make sure you update the associated comments. Future programmers will thank you for it.

There are even some formatting standards you can use when writing comments that can be picked up by other tools, such as your IDE or documentation-generation tools. These tools will take the code and its comments, and mix them so you can get a better understanding and not have to read and mentally parse the actual code.

Figure 2.1 shows an example. Notice how the tooltips generated by the same code differ when a properly formatted comment is added to the mix. That's JavaScript code, and the comments follow JSDoc standards (https://jsdoc.app/), which tell you how to format your comments so that a machine can parse them and get useful information from them. You can clearly identify things such as variable types and names, return types, descriptions, and more, and in this example, the IDE can parse it and show an informative tooltip.

Tooltip with JSDoc comments

```
(method) MySingleton.getInstance(): MySingleton

Returns the existing instance of the singleton. If there is no instance created, it creates
a new one for you.

@returns — The exsting instance
```

vs.

Tooltip without comments

```
(method) MySingleton.getInstance(): MySingleton
```

Figure 2.1   The effect of properly formatted comments in your IDE

There are comment formats for other languages too; this is not only for JavaScript. Make sure you look for these standards for the language you're using, and apply them to your commenting practices. They won't solve all your problems, but they will help quite a lot.

FOLLOWING PROJECT-WIDE STANDARDS

When you work with a team of developers, not everyone's code will follow the same standards unless you're all forced to. The language itself sets a syntax you need to follow, and maybe the framework you're using will force you to use one particular set of patterns in your code, but you still have a lot of wiggle room to add your own coding style. This would not be a problem if everyone on the team had a similar style, but there are so many aspects that can change from developer to developer that it can get messy unless someone sets a universal standard to follow.

There is a programming paradigm called "convention over configuration" that was made very popular by Ruby on Rails (http://rubyonrails.org/) back in the day. In essence, it means you should have sensible default behavior and only create specific code for a section of your logic if that expected default is not met. For example, consider a class representing a database table in your code. If that class is called "Notes," you'd expect the table to have the same name and your class to have one property for each field in the table (again, aptly named and typed). Only if that expectation is not met would you have to jump in and write the code to map the values or do whatever you need to make the class work with your internal logic and the database structure.

Why am I suddenly talking about convention over configuration? Because you should expect your team and your coding standards to work the same way. Reading a team member's code should feel like you're reading your own. This helps alleviate some of the cognitive load associated with parsing code to understand what it is trying to do. You should have a set of standards that cover style issues like the following:

- How to name your variables (for instance, always use English words and camel-case notation, or use specific prefixes to identify their type so readers don't have to look up their definition). This by itself is not enough to document your code, but it's a good starting point.
- How to perform specific minor tasks (such as always comparing two values with === instead of using == sometimes).
- The maximum length of a line of code (normally, coding standards limit the length to 80 characters, which corresponds to what terminals normally allow).
- How to name your files or where to save them (such as having a specific folder where all common code should live).

I could go on, but you get the point. These standards will keep you from having to make decisions about the basic tasks and will let you focus on the important job of solving your problem. Mind you, these standards can be very opinionated; after all, they're likely coming from a single person, such as your tech lead. But that's fine—you don't have to agree with them, you just have to use them, especially if you're joining the team after it's been working together for a while.

The good news is that there are tools known as "linters" that can help you check for these standards in your code. They're normally included in your IDE or can be configured to run on predeployment or premerge events, ensuring you're not sending code that doesn't follow the right conventions.

Coding standards are a great way of writing code that is easier for your team to read, even if that someone comes years after you, and you're no longer working for the company. Standards alone will not make all your code readable, but they will ensure that the reader is only faced with a single coding style rather than a mix of several.

A CASE FOR LITERATE PROGRAMMING

Remember when I said earlier that there is no such thing as self-documenting code? Well, hold my beer, because I'm about to go against my own words, kind of. Literate programming is a programming paradigm that allows you to write code and documentation at the same time.

Normally you would first write your code and then write the documentation based on it. You could, potentially, do the reverse and use the documentation as your development blueprints to create the code. However, with literate programming, you write both at the same time. You create an explanation of your logic and show snippets of your code. This documentation is then be processed, and actual working code is created and saved to one location, while a dynamic version of that documentation (normally an HTML version) is saved somewhere else.

Let's look at a quick example. Pretend you're building a JavaScript library meant to provide two functions: `mult` and `div` (multiplication and division). Following literate programming, you can write a document like the following.

Listing 2.2   The markup version of our documentation/source code

```
..      include:: <isoamsa.txt>
..      include:: <isopub.txt>

Introduction
-------------
This is a sample documentation for a very simple JavaScript function

MULT function
--------------
The MULT function requires two different parameters `a` and `b`,
both numbers ideally.

@o my-math-lib.js
@{
function mult(a, b) {
    return a * b
}
@}

DIV function
-------------
The DIV function takes care of dividing `a` with `b` whenever possible.

@o my-math-lib.js
@{
function divide(a, b) {
    @<validate parameters@>
    return a / b
}
@}

Value validation for the division
----------------------------------
Because one can't correctly divide a number by 0 (or a non-numeric or
undefined value for that matter) using JavaScript, the following
code takes care of checking for the value of `b`:

@d validate...
@{if(typeof b == "undefined" || isNaN(b) || b == 0) {
    return 0
}@}
```

As you can see, there is no one place where the code resides all together. Here I've split the code into three different chunks. Two are marked to be output to the same file (my-math-lib.js), while the third is marked as a code snippet so it can be included inside other sections.

The main benefit of this way of working is that you are forced to make a mental switch from only writing code (or only writing documentation)—you have to think about both at the same time. The end result, when done properly, is much richer documentation filled with examples, and the code is less prone to errors, since you've already thoroughly explained what it is meant to do.

Originally introduced by Donald Knuth around 1984, the literate programming paradigm is great for small coding projects. Normally you'd want to create detailed documentation filled with examples for things like libraries and tools that other developers will use. Those projects tend to be smaller than, say, creating the internal intranet for a whole company.

Here's how literate programming works:

1 You write everything using a markup language (depending on the implementation, it can be Markdown, Lex, or something similar).
2 You use specific custom tags across the text to signal elements such as code snippets, import statements (so you can split your writing into multiple files), and other elements that allow you to reuse blocks of text in different places.
3 You *weave* all the snippets together into the final source code.
4 You *tangle* the snippets and written documentation into an HTML file that will act as the user-facing documentation.

Don't worry too much about the weaving and tangling steps (the last two steps). They'll be taken care of by pyWeb (https://github.com/slott56/py-web-tool), which is the tool I'll use to parse the code from listing 2.2.

PyWeb generates two files: my-math-lib.js, which is full-on JavaScript without any extra documentation (see listing 2.3), and my-math-lib.html, which is the dynamic documentation (shown in figure 2.2, rendered as HTML).

Listing 2.3 Final version of our code, without any extra documentation

```
function mult(a, b) {
    return a * b
}

function divide(a, b) {
    if(typeof b == "undefined" || isNaN(b) || b == 0) {
      return 0
    }
    return a / b
}
```

The HTML is preformatted by default, but you can edit it and its stylesheet to make it look however you like. The point here is that the hardest part, which would be writing the actual HTML, is already done for you. Changing the styles to make it look better is a minor job in comparison.

Is this the answer to all our documentation problems? Will this programming paradigm change the way we work and write our code? I don't think so. Larger projects will still require a focus on the code and folder structure that literate programming can't provide. Smaller projects, though, such as libraries and small frameworks, can take advantage of literate programming without their coding workflow changing that much. It's definitely an interesting alternative that's compatible with all programming languages, and it's a great option if you're looking to save some time writing documentation.

Introduction

This is a sample documentation for a very simple JavaScript function

MULT function

The MULT function requiress two different parameters *a* and *b*, both numbers ideally.

my-math-lib.js (1) =

```
function mult(a, b) {
    return a * b
}
```

◊ *my-math-lib.js (1).*

DIV function

The DIV function takes care of dividing *a* with *b* whenever possible.

my-math-lib.js (2) +=

```
function   divide(a, b) {
    →validate parameters (3)
    return a / b
}
```

◊ *my-math-lib.js (2).*

Value validation for division

Because one can't correctly divide a number by 0 (or a non-numeric or undefined value for that matter) using JavaScript, the following code takes care of checking for the value of *b*:

validate parameters (3) =

```
if(typeof b == "undefined" || isNaN(b) || b == 0) {
    return 0
}
```

◊ *validate parameters (3).* Used by: my-math-lib.js (2)

Figure 2.2   The tangled version of the documentation, mixing code and comments

2.2.2   *Readable code > one-liners*

Documentation in all its forms is crucial to helping people understand how code works, but there is also something to be said about the way you write your code. Sometimes a single line of code can require several paragraphs of documentation because it's so optimized and minified that mentally parsing it takes too long. That is plain unacceptable in most situations.

Unless you're writing embedded code for very resource-constrained devices, saving characters while writing will not yield huge benefits. Consider, instead, writing the solution for human beings and machines alike—code that works but that is a lot easier to read. The following listing shows an example of what I mean.

Listing 2.4   Readable vs. optimized code

```
salaries = {
  "You": 100000,
  "Sarah Connor": 90000,
  "John Doe": 100000,
  "Laura Micheals": 60000,
  "Mike Tyson": 35000
}

def who_makes_the_most():
  dict_sal = salaries.copy()
  high_sal = 0
  for name in dict_sal:
    dict_sal[name] = dict_sal[name]
    if dict_sal[name] > high_sal:
      high_sal = dict_sal[name]

  high_paid_emp = []
  for name in dict_sal:
    if dict_sal[name] == high_sal:
      high_paid_emp.append(name)

  return high_paid_emp

def who_makes_the_most_v2():
  return [emp for emp in salaries if salaries[emp] == max([sal for sal in
    salaries.values()])]

print who_makes_the_most()
print who_makes_the_most_v2()
```

Version 1 calculates who makes the most money at the company. This version is very verbose and understandable.

Version 2 calculates who makes the most money with a reduced and harder-to-read function.

Both versions of the function in listing 2.4 will yield the same result, but one requires a single line of code while the other uses 11. Is version 2 better than the original? This is a very subjective question to answer. A team of expert Python developers with many years of experience will not need a lot of time to read the one-line function. However, if someone new comes in with the intention of editing or expanding on it, that person will face some issues. That's not only because the function itself is a lot harder to understand; the fact that it's been reduced to a single line with the same amount of functionality means the complexity has been packed into very specific constructs.

In this example, there are two list-comprehension expressions nested and a call to the max function. Suppose we want to add logic to this code to uppercase the names and remove the first names from the returned values. We'll have to expand the one-line function. This will make the code harder to read, and it will be harder to add an inline check for scenarios where there are no last names. The following listing shows how the functions grow, based on this added complexity.

Listing 2.5 Example from listing 2.4 expanded with added logic

```
def who_makes_the_most():
  dict_sal = salaries.copy()           Version 1, with extra
  high_sal = 0                         logic added into it
  for name in dict_sal:
    dict_sal[name] = dict_sal[name]
    if dict_sal[name] > high_sal:
      high_sal = dict_sal[name]

  high_paid_emp = []
  for name in dict_sal:
    if dict_sal[name] == high_sal:
      name_parts = name.upper().split(' ')
      if len(name_parts) == 2:
        high_paid_emp.append(name_parts[1])
      else:
        high_paid_emp.append(name_parts[0])

  return high_paid_emp
                                       Version 2 of the same function
                                       turned into a longer line
def who_makes_the_most_v2():
  return [emp.split(' ')[-1].upper() for emp in salaries if salaries[emp]
  ➥ == max([sal for sal in salaries.values()])]
```

You can see how the code in version 1 of the function remains a lot easier to mentally parse. You now have a clear place where you're checking whether there are last names or not and what to do when there aren't. With the one-liner, however, we've resorted to using index -1, which references the first element starting from the end of the list (in other words, the last element). This works, but using negative indexes on arrays is something not everyone is comfortable with, and it requires that you understand how Python deals with them. Again, both functions do the same thing, but even in this basic example, we're having to manually translate the packed logic instead of just reading it.

The longer version 1 function could be simplified, of course, and still be more readable than version 2. However, the point here is to show you both extremes. You shouldn't aim for either—you should aim for something in between, like the following listing.

Listing 2.6 A new version, capturing the best of both worlds

```
def who_makes_the_most_v3():
  dict_sal = salaries.copy()
  high_sal = max(dict_sal.values())

  high_paid_emp = []
  for name in dict_sal:
    if dict_sal[name] == high_sal:
      name_parts = name.upper().split(' ')
```

```
  if len(name_parts) == 2:
    high_paid_emp.append(name_parts[1])
  else:
    high_paid_emp.append(name_parts[0])

return high_paid_emp
```

In this version, we get rid of the first `for` loop, since the `max` function already does that for us. But we've kept the expanded version of the more complex section of our logic intact because it's a lot easier to read that way.

With that said, you just have to remember one thing: readable code does not substitute for documentation, they complement each other. You will still have to document your algorithms and explain why you're doing what you're doing. However, writing readable code makes it unnecessary to document some sections in detail, thus saving you a bit of time.

Writing understandable code is no excuse for overcomplicating a solution, however. While trying to make your code easy to read, you'll also want to avoid a very common trap: overengineering.

2.3 *Overengineering: The first capital sin*

Overengineering is the "art" of creating overly complex solutions for simple problems. And trust me, it will work against you by slowing you down and increasing the time you and your team take to finish a feature.

Imagine you need to add some code to your newly developed login feature. You took your time, but the login page is working well and everyone's happy about it. However, you never added any logging to it, so you can't tell what's happening behind the scenes. How would you tackle this problem? Would you write a few lines of code that solve your problem right now (let's call it a *greedy solution* because you're only worried about today's problem) or would you create a component that can be used by your entire team now and in the future, and potentially even in other projects?

This is a very common question you'll face in your day-to-day activities. There is always a chance that your work can be reused if you write it with that goal in mind. But then again, the greedy approach is almost always faster, because you're only thinking about your particular use case and needs.

2.3.1 *Spotting a case of overengineering*

The elegance of overengineering can keep you from realizing you're falling into the trap until it's too late. Cases of overengineering are usually easier to spot from outside—if you're not the one writing the code, it's a lot easier to see what's happening. While you're on the inside, you're working under the assumption that you're creating something perfect that will work no matter what.

I'm not saying you'll always be wrong—the code you're writing could be perfect—but you should be asking yourself whether the effort is worth it. It's a simple question, but to correctly answer it, you'll need to step back, consider the context you're working in (the project's needs, the timeline, who else depends on your work, and other factors) and answer objectively. You can't fall in love with your work—that's the first step into overengineering. Save that for your own time and your own personal projects, when there is no deadline looming around the corner.

So, is your effort worth it? You're essentially working extra to complete a task that would already have been finished. That's acceptable if your extra effort yields extra value (such as a more robust implementation, a library that everyone can use to save time later, etc.), but will it? Or are you solving your problem with a solution that is not really required?

Back to our login example, logging is something that most frameworks and languages already solve. Yes, you can add code on top of those solutions to create something majestic, but we're back to the same question: is it worth it?

Logging is used to find out what's causing a problem or a strange behavior that can't be understood from the user-facing side. In other words, if used wisely, it can serve as a backdoor to the inner workings of your logic. But there are many ways of achieving the same goal:

- You can log your messages to the standard output and have your runtime capture and save it. This is a great solution if you're working with a quick script (a scheduled task that runs every once in a while and performs basic operations). It's not great if you're working with a distributed microservice-based architecture, because this would create a log file on every server, requiring you to manually jump from server to server. That's probably the worst nightmare for someone trying to troubleshoot a problem with these logs.
- You can centralize the logs on a single server, which simplifies the task of browsing through them, but it makes your logging code a lot more complex. You now have to worry about sending information to another server, and there needs to be something that handles concurrency on the other side. Big architectures are a great fit for this use case, but because the information saved can grow exponentially, browsing through it can become a daunting task. Think about trying to open and read a 100 GB log file.
- You can implement a centralized, searchable solution in the cloud, so you'll never run out of disk space. With a solution like this, you can save all your logs in a single place and go through them quickly and easily. You're not only solving your problem, you're solving everyone's logging problems. However, you're now implementing two solutions: one on your original logging system, and one to actually store and search through that information.

There are thousands of other ways of implementing a logging solution. These are just three that show how easily a solution can escalate to the point where it becomes a textbook case of overengineering. You can't possibly say that the last solution doesn't sound good, and if you're on the team working on it, you're probably thinking you're solving the company's logging problems for the next five years. However, if you're the manager looking at it from outside, you'll be thinking about how the timeline is growing due to this magnificent solution, and you'll be asking the "Is this really worth it?" question even in your sleep.

How can you avoid falling for the overengineering trap? Easy: think like your manager. I know that's easier said than done, especially if you're starting out in your career, so let me break it down. Every time you're faced with a problem to solve, you'll essentially go through these two phases:

1   *You'll create a mental model of a solution*—This is just a fancy way of saying that you'll figure out how to solve it. This mental model doesn't have to involve coding or a particular framework. This can be a high-level idea of how everything needs to connect to reach the desired outcome.

2   *You'll start coding it*—There's nothing fancy about this phase. You'll implement the high-level solution by turning it into code.

The way to avoid overengineering is to add a step right in between those two:

1.5   Stop and think objectively. Mentally step away from your idea, look at the bigger picture, think about the current state of your project, and ask yourself the following questions: "What else is everyone working on?" "Who else will benefit from the perfect solution I just came up with?" "Does anyone else need to benefit from this solution?"

There will be times when your great idea is well received and it will have a valid business case, so it'll make sense to spend extra time to create it. But by looking at it from afar, you'll be able to assess whether or not you're creating a second problem instead of a solution.

If you were to ask yourself those questions for this particular example, maybe you would have noticed that the third, cloud, solution was just too much. Maybe your actual solution should land somewhere between the first and second solutions.

Overengineering is not the only common problem found in our ranks. There is also a big mystery that most of us run into during our career: the random bug mystery.

2.4   *The random bug mystery*

Software and computers are deterministic in nature. Given the same input, every piece of code will always yield the same output no matter where or when you run it (unless you go the extra mile to produce random results). But that's still not enough to keep developers from thinking some bugs are random.

Truth is, there are no random bugs, there are only bugs. Some of them seem like they've been sent to us directly from the depths of hell, but that changes nothing. Your job as a developer is to fix them. But learning how to spot and fix bugs is not a simple task. I like to think of it as an art that takes years to perfect.

Step one is to understand the truth about bugs: they come from you, the developer. Step two is to understand why they're happening. That is where the root cause analysis (RCA) comes in. An RCA is an analysis done to understand three main things:

why something is happening, how you can solve it, and, ideally, what you can do to prevent it from happening again.

Let's go back to our login page example. Suppose we have a bug report from a user stating the following:

> The days it's my turn to take the dog out in the morning, when I'm back and I try to log in to your system, sometimes it takes a couple of minutes and I have to try a few times. In fact, even after a slow login, the system seems to be quite unstable and I need to keep refreshing the page.

Reproduction steps:

1 Log in with my username and password.
2 That's it.

Your team has been trying to fix the problem, but the very first step in solving any bug is yet to be finished: reproducing the bug. You're all perfectly capable of logging in to your system, and you're not really seeing any issues while navigating through the site. You can't solve a bug if you can't reproduce it 100% of the time, which is why you can't really do much if you get a bug report without any reproduction steps. Bug reproduction steps will give you a better idea of what components your user is interacting with, and thus give you a clue about where to start your debugging work. How can you tackle such a bug report, considering there is no concise and sure way to reproduce it?

2.4.1 *Performing a root cause analysis (RCA)*

However you approach RCAs, remember to always focus on these three key questions:

- *Why is it happening?* Your number one objective needs to be understanding why the bug is happening. If you can't achieve this, there is no point in moving forward.
- *How can you solve it?* Your RCA needs to include the actions required to solve the problem. Normally, understanding why it's happening leads to the beginning of the solution. If you figure out your bug is caused by *A*, the initial solution will be to keep *A* from happening.
- *How can you keep it from happening again?* It's not enough to fix the issue; you also need to make sure it never happens again. And no, they're not the same thing. To give you a simple example, a bug could be caused by a problem in a record on your database, and fixing it could be as simple as updating that record. But what caused that record to have that particular value? How can you be sure that, after updating that record manually, it won't happen again? That's when this step comes into play. If you have two linked problems, one being the root cause of the other, you'll need to go deeper than a shallow fix to find the real root cause of your problem.

There are many ways of doing an RCA, so I'll keep it simple and tell you about my "Five Whys" approach (or as I like to call it, "How my kids perform an RCA"). The idea behind this method is to think like a 6-year-old and ask "Why did this happen?" Have you ever had to answer that question from a kid? Mine is around that age right now, and every time I answer that question, he doesn't even blink before asking the immediate follow-up: "OK, but why?" That's what this method is based on: keep asking "why" until you're satisfied. Statistically speaking, by the fifth "why," you should have all the answers you need.

Let's try it with our example, assuming we've exchanged a few emails with our customer and we've figured out that he takes the dog out at around 5 a.m. some days during the week:

1 *Why is the logging service slow sometimes during the early hours of the morning?* Because the server appears to have fewer available resources during those hours.

2 *Why does the server sometimes have fewer resources during the early hours of the morning?* Because we perform a backup of our entire database every two weeks from 1 a.m. to 7 a.m.

3 *Why do we perform our database backup during those specific hours?* Because when we set it up, no one told us when to do it, so we just picked a time we assumed would have the least amount of traffic. We never checked the stats to confirm our assumption.

4 *Why does our database backup process take so long to finish?* Because we have four different databases right now, and they're all being backed up at the same time.

5 *Why can't we perform smaller, incremental backups every day to minimize the load on our servers?* I ... I don't know, that's actually a great idea!

Granted, this is a made-up "random" bug, but you get the point. We could have stopped at the third "why," because by then we already had our answer: it was a timing issue, and we needed to reschedule the backup process. However, by stopping there we would have found a subpar solution. It would have solved the immediate problem, but it couldn't fulfill the third goal of the RCA: to make sure it never happens again. Because we kept asking "why," by the fifth time we had identified more problems with the backup process and we had come up with a better solution.

The best part was that we were able to prove it wasn't a random bug after all. It wasn't even a bug with our code. This is also important to keep in mind: when you're conducting the RCA, remember to look outside the box. In this case, it involved asking the right question: "Why is the logging service slow?" I could have asked "Why is our code randomly malfunctioning," but I didn't. I went with the user's bug report instead of adding my own bias to the mix.

That's the key: you can't be doing an RCA with a solution to the problem in your mind. If you think you already know the answer to the problem, your questions will be geared toward proving that theory. You have to keep your investigation objective.

2.5   *You have to aim to be a developer*

To keep you from hindering your own professional progress (as well as your technical progress) you have to remember that you're a software developer, and that the technology you're using at any particular time is nothing but a tool. This may seem obvious, but sometimes companies put developers inside boxes to help them figure out who should work on what.

For example, imagine you're working as part of a team of five developers: you, John, Mike, Laura, and Sarah. Table 2.1 shows how easy it is to box you into a predefined role.

Table 2.1   **Understanding how you can be boxed in by the tasks you do**

Developer	Usual tasks	Box
You	Frontend coding, some CSS, JavaScript with React and a little bit of Vue (sometimes on some other projects)	Frontend dev, knows React and Vue
John	Frontend, always works on React	Frontend dev, knows React
Mike	Backend services, works with Java	Backend dev, knows Java
Laura	Backend services written in Java	Backend dev, knows Java
Sarah	Backend storage services, works with Java and MySQL	Backend dev, knows Java

Some developers, especially those who are new and have only worked for one company, will tend to believe that's the extent of their skills. In this example, you were placed inside a frontend developer box, which means you're stuck working with JavaScript for the foreseeable future. You can do a lot of things with JavaScript, but by letting others box you into a role, you're accepting that you can't learn from other languages that aren't frontend specific. That's a huge problem.

You've probably heard the statement, "If you only have a hammer, everything looks like a nail." It's a phrase normally attributed to Abraham Maslow in 1966, and it's said to be related to Maslow's law (also known as the law of the instrument), a cognitive bias involving overreliance on a particular instrument. This is all to say that someone actually sat down and considered the utility of knowing about multiple tools for performing what is seemingly the same job.

In the software development world, we can apply the same concept: if you only work with React, you'll think all your problems can be solved using reactive programming. Or if Java is all you know, you'll always try to create bloated solutions to potentially simple problems (apologies to Java developers—this is my own bias). Even if you're working with React from 9 to 6 every weekday, you'll see a lot of benefit by studying and working with other languages and frameworks. You're a developer, after all, not a React developer or a Java developer. You have to aim to be "just" a developer.

It took me quite a while to realize this, but once I stopped working with PHP (which took me five years) and made the leap into Ruby, which then led to Python and then to Node.js, I understood that all these languages have a lot of things in common. After jumping from technology to technology, I was able to step back and see the big picture: it's not about the language you're using, it's about the abstract concepts you're working with. That's why this book is not focused on one particular technology. It's not about learning how to be a Java developer everyone wants to work with—it's about being a great developer, with no tags attached.

All languages have loops and control statements. Some of them will let you use concepts such as classes to represent abstractions, while others will do the same thing through functions, but the same concepts will be there. Understanding this will yield two major benefits:

- *You can jump from language to language*—Once you know one programming paradigm, you can work with all languages that follow it. For example, you can jump from Java to C# and quickly pick up the syntactic differences. If you understand how functional programming works, you can jump from Lisp to Haskell with minimum effort. Focusing on the high-level abstractions all languages work with (their underlying paradigm) will help you change technologies, and potentially jobs, a lot faster. This will also make you a more flexible developer in the eyes of your managers (which is always a plus).

- *You can translate concepts from one language to another*—This is, to me, is the biggest benefit. Focusing only on the language you use every day will narrow the range of options you have when trying to solve a problem or to implement a new feature. You'll be learning from tutorials, books, and videos about the same language you're already familiar with, and you'll see the same techniques applied over and over under the same paradigm. However, learning about other languages, especially if they're quite different from the one you normally use, will help you see how others solve the same problems from a completely different point of view. Imagine working with JavaScript and learning about functional programming by reading about Lisp. Those are two completely different languages, but most of the concepts you'll learn from Lisp can be translated back to JavaScript, expanding the way you work with your everyday language. The same can be said for Python and Java, two seemingly different languages. Java developers might not be used to working with lambdas, but Python developers are—and Python solutions that involve lambdas might force you to take a second look at how lambdas work in Java.

One piece of advice I try to give to every developer is to get out of the box they're placed in by their day-to-day work. That's your comfort zone, and you can only grow once you move out of it. Even experienced developers can fall into the specialization trap, thinking that if they focus on a single piece of tech, they'll become master developers on it. (Find a COBOL developer and ask them how many options they have right now in the market.) Yes, they'll know everything about their particular framework or language, but they'll be lacking the variation and originality that come from knowing about other languages and how the same problem can be solved in different ways.

Remember that the underlying job of a developer is to solve problems. The language you use is just a tool, and all problems are different. You have to use the right tool for each problem. While you're at it, remember that languages aren't your only tools. Some take the shape of patterns or best practices. SOLID, DRY, and other acronyms represent such tools. Learn to love them, because you'll be around them for a while.

2.6   *SOLID, DRY, and other funny terms*

The last bit of advice I want to impart regarding coding is to keep these funny words in mind. While it might sound strange, our industry manages to use the strangest words to represent some of the best coding practices. In this section, I'm going to quickly cover some generic best practices that you'll be able to use with any language. However, I encourage you to always be on the lookout for best practices specific to the technology you're using, since there are always exceptions and particular practices that don't translate to other languages.

You don't need to memorize what I'll discuss in this section, but you should keep these terms and practices in the back of your mind when you're coding to ensure you're writing quality code.

2.6.1   *SOLID: Making your code strong as a rock*

SOLID is a group of principles that work together to provide great, clean, and readable code that is easy to extend and reuse. The following principles make up SOLID:

- Single responsibility principle
- Open-closed principle
- Liskov substitution principle
- Interface segregation principle
- Dependency inversion principle

Some of these might sound like complex programming theory concepts, but that's just the names. They make a lot of sense when you look at them from a practical point of view.

SINGLE RESPONSIBILITY PRINCIPLE

The idea behind the single responsibility principle is that any piece of code you abstract into a function should only focus on one task.

For instance, the Linux CLI tool `cat` can only read the content of a file and output it to standard output; the `wc` tool can only count the words of anything it reads from standard input. Individually these tools don't do much, but you can combine them to quickly count the words inside a file.

> **Listing 2.7   Combining simple tools to obtain more complex behavior**

```
$ cat myfile.txt | wc -w
```

This is a principle that Unix-based systems (such as Linux and macOS) take to heart. Any command-line tool in these systems only does one thing and is able to receive as input the output of another tool. This provides a great deal of flexibility, because you can use them as building blocks and compose several to create new, more complex behavior.

Your code should aim for the same sort of *complex simplicity* that this principle proposes. Make sure your functions focus on a single task and that, if required, they can be combined to create more complex output. This is to say, the moment you find yourself with a function named getUserAndRelatedRecords that contains logic for all these steps, you should stop. Move each step into an individual function, and make sure getUserAndRelatedRecords only orchestrates those functions. This provides two main benefits:

- Functions are shorter, which makes them a lot easier to explain, document, change, and maintain.
- Combining functions is much easier than writing a mega function with all the mixed logic.

Remember to aim for small functions as much as you can. This will help you keep your code SOLID without even trying.

OPEN-CLOSED PRINCIPLE

The open-closed principle suggests that you should design your components to be open to extensibility but closed to modification. I know it reads like a tongue twister, but it's a lot easier than it sounds. When you're designing a new component (be it a package, a class, or a function), you should expect anyone who wants to add to its functionality to properly extend it and not to modify it.

This means that if those who want to extend your code must modify the source, you're making their life a lot harder. Not only that, but you're providing a terrible developer experience. Any code you provide to others (whether in the form of a module or a list of functions) should have the needs of your users (other developers) in mind.

The following listing shows an example. If you were to provide this class to other developers, and they wanted to expand on the list of valid cities, they would have to change its source code.

Listing 2.8 **Example of a poorly designed class**

```
class CitiesValidator {         # This list is fixed and not easy to extend
  knownCities = ["Madrid", "Barcelona", "New York"]

  isAValidCity(cityName) {
    return this.knownCities.indexOf(cityName) != -1
  }
}
```

However, if you were to restructure the class from listing 2.8 to allow developers to add new valid cities, like in listing 2.9, your code would be following best practices.

Listing 2.9   A valid open-closed code enabling extensibility

```
class CitiesValidator {
  knownCities = ["Madrid", "Barcelona", "New York"]

  isAValidCity(cityName) {
    return this.knownCities.indexOf(cityName) != -1
  }

  addValidCity(city) {    # Through this method you can expand
      # the list without editing it
       this.knownCities.add(city)
  }
}
```

Open-closed code is a lot easier to extend, which is something you should always be aiming for. This is especially relevant when you're working as part of a team and your code needs to be used by others.

LISKOV SUBSTITUTION PRINCIPLE

Liskov's substitution principle is not simple to follow because there is really no formula to apply. You have to take into consideration the purpose of your abstraction. The best way to think of this principle is, "If it quacks like a duck, moves like a duck, looks like a duck, but it needs battery, then you probably have the wrong abstraction." That's the whole point of the Liskov substitution principle—to ensure you're properly abstracting your concepts, and that if you decide to make one inherit from another, that you're going about it the correct way.

Inheritance is one of the most basic tools of any object-oriented programming paradigm, but developers tend to overuse inheritance instead of looking for more suitable alternatives. For example, imagine setting up a Square class that inherits from Rectangle. While geometrically speaking that might be correct, the setWidth and setHeight methods of the Square class will make little sense, considering that one method would have to call the other to ensure both dimensions have the same value. If you created the inheritance because you wanted to reuse code, there are better ways to do so (such as function composition) that would yield the same benefits and would make more sense from a programming standpoint.

This is all to say that you should make sure your code makes semantic sense. After all, you're representing concepts, and the way they relate to each other should be as important as the fact that your code works. That will ensure it's easier for others to maintain and understand.

INTERFACE SEGREGATION PRINCIPLE

The interface segregation principle focuses on the interface you export to external users. In object-oriented programming, you have a concept known as the interface, which helps create a contract for your classes—you can define what methods and properties are mandatory for any developer wanting to implement it. This principle says that when you're creating these interfaces, you should make sure you only define outward-facing methods and keep the internal logic hidden. In other words, don't force developers to implement the same helper methods you did. As long as they keep the public interface (the public methods) the same, the way they implement them is up to them.

In fact, you can take this concept a bit further and consider segregating optional behavior in a separate interface that developers would only use if they need it. The following listing shows a simple example. Pretend you're trying to define the interface for an abstraction of a plane (maybe you're working on a video game or a simulator).

Listing 2.10   A bloated interface forcing the implementation of unnecessary methods

```
interface IPlane {
    move(speed: number);
    fly();
    touchDown();
    waterLanding()
}
```

The waterLanding method is only required if you're implementing a seaplane; otherwise, that method is not required. Why would you force anyone trying to represent a plane of any type to implement such a particular method?

The next method follows the interface segregation principle and solves this little design issue.

Listing 2.11   Properly segregated interfaces and an example of their use

```
interface IPlane {
    move(speed: number);
    fly();
    touchDown();
}

interface ILandsOnWater{
    waterLanding()
}

class MyPlanes implements IPlane, ILandsOnWater {
    waterLanding() {
        throw new Error("Method not implemented.");
    }
    move(speed: number) {
        throw new Error("Method not implemented.");
    }
    fly() {
        throw new Error("Method not implemented.");
    }
```

```
touchDown() {
    throw new Error("Method not implemented.");
}

}
```

You can see how the `MyPlanes` class uses both interfaces. You could opt out of the `ILandsOnWater` interface to implement a normal plane class as well. That's completely up to the developer and their needs. That's what good design means: giving developers choices that make sense and that simplify their lives.

Granted, the interface segregation principle implies a bit more code. While it can be easy to confuse *more* code with *bloated* code, you have to remember that it's all about balance. Having no design is bad, but excessive design is also a bad thing. There is no formula for understanding when to stop adding patterns and classes; you'll get a feel for that over time.

DEPENDENCY INVERSION PRINCIPLE

As developers, we need to deal with dependencies all the time. It's not practical or possible in most real-world scenarios to implement something completely from scratch and as a single entity. Even if you're the only one working on your code, you'll normally feel the need to modularize it, extract bits into separate files, and treat those as dependencies as well. The dependency inversion principle is essentially a guideline for object-oriented programming scenarios, and it dictates that any entity you create should depend on a higher level of abstraction. The definition is a bit generic, I know, but that's the whole point. You have to generalize your dependencies, which in turn will let you switch them around when required.

Consider interfaces (since we used them previously) to live at a higher level of abstraction than classes. If you have a dependency between two classes, by directly referencing them you're coupling them and their implementations together. If instead you were to use interfaces to reference "types of classes," you could reference them and then exchange multiple classes that implement the same interface. This would decouple the implementations while still allowing you to keep the relationship alive.

Suppose you're working on the login process we've been discussing throughout this chapter. You have to implement a function that reads from the database and validates the credentials provided. The following listing shows a very coupled implementation. What would you say is wrong with it?

Listing 2.12 **Direct dependency coupling two pieces of code**

```
//...
checkCredentials(username: string, password: string,
sqlReader: SQLReader,          logger: FileLogger): boolean {

    let result = sqlReader.checkCredentials(username, password)
    if(result) {
        return true
```

```
    } else {
        logger.error("Error, username and password are invalid")
        return false
    }
}
```

This example shows very clearly how our function's code is coupled with two dependencies: `SQLReader` and `FileLogger`. This means the implementation of our method is dependent on the implementation of these classes—if they change, we'll need to change our code. That's not a great design, especially if we don't control the code of those dependencies.

Even if those implementations don't change, our requirements might, forcing us either to get the data from somewhere else (for example, from an external API) or to save our logs to a database instead of a file, either of which would force us to change our implementation. In either of those cases, our core logic wouldn't change; we would just need to use different dependencies. If we had a way to ensure the contract with those dependencies, we could switch the implementations with others that follow the same contract, and our code would not need to change.

Enter the dependency inversion principle (also known as DIP). By using higher-order entities (interfaces in this case), we could define the contract for our dependencies, thus allowing us to easily change them up in the future. The following listing shows how much more elegant the code looks and feels, now that it offers you the flexibility to decide which dependencies to use.

Listing 2.13 Using interfaces to avoid coupling classes

```
interface ICredentialsChecker {
    checkCredentials(usr: string, pwd: string);
}

interface ILogger {
    error(msg: string);
    info(msg: string);
    warn(msg: string)
}

//...
checkCredentials(username: string, password: string,
                 credChecker: ICredentialsChecker,
logger: ILogger): boolean {

    let result = credChecker.checkCredentials(username, password)
    if(result) {
        return true
    } else {
        logger.error("Error, username and password are invalid")
        return false
    }
}
```

Congrats, you've successfully decoupled `sqlReader` and `FileLogger` from your implementation. As long as they implement the corresponding interfaces (`ICredentials-Checker` and `ILogger`), they'll work. If tomorrow you need to change the logger, just make the new one implement the same `ILogger` interface, and you won't have to do anything else. That's a huge win.

Granted, this principle might increase the complexity of bigger codebases and the cognitive load required to mentally parse the code. That's not ideal, so you'll have to find a balance between coupling code and limiting flexibility and complexity. There is no hard rule here that you can follow. Everything covered so far in this section should give you the tools you need to make that decision.

2.6.2 *KISS your code*

KISS is an acronym for "Keep It Simple Stupid" (or its less offensive variant, "Keep It Stupid Simple"). However you read it, the point of this principle is to avoid complexity as much as possible. Sound familiar? Overengineering is such a big problem for developers that we created a fun little acronym to remind us to avoid it.

Granted, complexity has its place in systems design, and it is definitely something you'll need in situations where there is no simple solution. But that's not what I'm talking about here—complexity and overengineering are two very different things:

- Complexity is acceptable (even desirable) when you're trying to do something that not many people have attempted. For common tasks, you'll normally have your choice of multiple solutions in different libraries and frameworks abstracting your problem. For example, tasks such as querying a database, logging a user into your system, and saving error logs in a safe place are tasks we have to deal with almost every day. You'll need a very strong reason to add complexity to those tasks instead of using existing solutions. However, if you're trying to send a rocket to Mars and have it reenter the atmosphere with a controlled descent (something that right now only a single company has successfully achieved), your design and internal architecture will likely be complex. That's perfectly fine.
- Overengineering is adding complexity to solve a simple problem. As I mentioned earlier, the best way to spot it is through the eyes of experience. If you're just starting out and don't have much experience, you should take advantage of practices like code review, where other developers will read your code and provide feedback. You can also ask more experienced developers—take advantage of their years of experience and learn from them.

Complexity and overengineering can be confused, but they aren't the same thing. And while the KISS principle is intended to have you avoid complexity like the plague, you should remember that sometimes there is no way around it. You should not be afraid to add complexity to your code as long as you don't overdo it.

2.6.3 *Keep your code DRY*

Here's a good rule of thumb to follow when writing code: if you're doing something more than once, it needs to be abstracted. In other words, *don't repeat yourself* (DRY). The purpose of this principle is to remind you that while it might be easier to just copy and paste a block of code from one place to another, that's not the best solution. Note that I'm talking about duplicating a piece of code here; it is perfectly fine to copy, paste, and then change a piece of code to get a head start on writing your code.

A block of code, a piece of logic, a section of your internal architecture—this principle applies to every portion of software development. As you start gaining experience and seeing different projects and technologies, you'll start seeing patterns, common behaviors, and tasks that can be abstracted. As a developer, that will give you the tools to understand how to best apply this principle to your code.

Abstracting can mean anything, from creating a shared function with code that was repeated in multiple files to rewriting a bit of your logic in a new class and encapsulating sections of behavior that can be reused somewhere else. Think about it this way: As a developer, you'll always want to do the least amount of work. You have to think about the long term though, because it might look easier to duplicate or triplicate a piece of code in the short term. In the long run, when you have to maintain that code, fix a bug, add a feature, or change a value, you'll have to remember exactly where you repeated that code. If it's abstracted in a single location, you'll only have to fix it once. That's the main advantage of this principle.

The DRY principle can be applied to almost any situation. Are you looking at a UML diagram and seeing similar classes everywhere? Maybe you can abstract the common pattern into a single class that others can inherit from. Are you working on a third project in your company and finding yourself pulling code from the previous two because you always consume an internal API? Chances are you can abstract that code and share it as a common library that you and future projects can take advantage of. The DRY principle doesn't just apply to the scope of a single project or even to code—it's about seeing repeating patterns in your day-to-day life and trying to abstract them so that others can reuse them.

2.6.4 *YAGNI, another funny word*

I already explained why early optimization is a bad practice and why you should focus on your current needs and worry about optimizing your code once it's working. The YAGNI principle, an acronym for "You Ain't Gonna Need It," addresses a very similar concept: you shouldn't build features you don't currently need. This is not a code-specific principle; instead, it's more related to a very common way of working in our industry: agile development.

Agile is a way of working that allows you to quickly iterate over an idea, adjust course based on feedback, and move forward. It has proven to be a great tool for combating older practices like Waterfall, where you'd spend months designing the entire system and then more months building it until it can see the light of day at the end of the process. Don't get me wrong, Waterfall is still very relevant in some situations, but your time to market—how fast you can get a first version of your product out—is much lower when you take an agile approach.

Many companies work with agile methodologies for this reason, and a part of this process is to have a big-picture backlog of work, which allows you to understand everything you're planning on doing in the long term. In the shorter term, you'd normally plan exactly how you're going to achieve the next iteration of work (usually known as a "sprint"). There is always the temptation within a team of developers to look way ahead at future features—you know the feature will eventually come, since it's already in the backlog. But what YAGNI tells you is that, given the changing nature of an agile project and the quick turnaround you can have, given early feedback after one iteration, future features could potentially disappear from the backlog. Code you created in anticipation of a future feature may no longer be required.

This is why a good rule of thumb when working on an agile project is to always stick to the needs of your current sprint. Worry about implementing solutions for coming features when it's time to work on them, and not sooner. You can plan how the overall system will fit together, but don't spend time implementing anything that's not set in stone, because you might not need it later.

Summary

- Good code beats perfect code every time. Good code is enough to deploy a working feature to production, and you can iterate on it and improve it later. Holding out for perfect code is a waste of time trying to achieve an impossible goal.
- Optimizing code is only required once you know your code works, not before. Otherwise, you're optimizing based on assumptions, and you may be focusing on the wrong areas of your code.
- Bad code can be a great starting point. You can later improve it, change it, and optimize it as much as you need.
- Documenting your code is a must, no matter how you do it. Otherwise, neither you nor anybody else reading your code will understand it in three months.
- Be aware of the overengineering trap and avoid it. Otherwise, you'll end up wasting time writing a feature that's prepared for use cases that will never happen.
- There are no random bugs, period. Every problem with your product has an RCA, and if you intend to fix the bug, you'll have to find it.
- Be a developer and avoid the specialization trap. Keep learning about new technologies and trying new things. That way, you'll avoid being put into a box, and you can stay updated and relevant within our industry.
- Remember to KISS your code and DRY your SOLID designs as much as you can. In other words, avoid repeated code (DRY), try to keep your designs as simple as possible (KISS), use dependency inversion whenever possible, and make sure your functions only do one thing and do it right (SOLID). Most importantly, follow as many best practices listed in this chapter as possible.

Unit testing: delivering code that works

This chapter covers

- Why unit tests are important
- What parts of your codebase to test and what parts to ignore
- How to test your code using dependency injection, mocks, stubs, and more
- When to create the tests during the development workflow

Unit testing is one of those tasks that all junior developers are assigned, especially when they first join an existing project. It is expected that they get familiar with the source code as soon as possible. The problem, though, is that the purpose of unit testing is to provide security and certainty over the stability of your code so you know it's bug-free after you change it. Unit testing is not intended to help you understand a codebase. Furthermore, a junior developer entering a team is not the ideal person to write these tests. They don't know the code or the features they're testing, so how can they truly cover every use case and edge case?

As you'll see in this chapter, unit tests are an incredibly unappreciated tool that can give you certainty over the validity of the code you write. But to ensure that, you have to know the code you're testing and understand what it needs to do. This chapter won't offer a "how-to" guide on writing unit tests because this book is language agnostic, and every language has its own frameworks and tools. However, the concepts I'll cover here are generic and valid for all languages. Even if you're not familiar with the code in my examples, you should be able to extrapolate the principles to your language of choice by looking for the keywords I'll be using.

In this chapter, I want to cover the noncoding aspects of unit tests:

- Why should you unit test your code?
- How do you unit test your code?
- What should you test?
- When should you test?

With the answers to these four questions, you'll leave this chapter understanding the true power behind the practice of unit testing, and you'll be ready to apply these principles in your language of choice.

3.1   *Why unit test your code?*

This is not a question we tend to ask ourselves. You probably either consider unit tests to be part of your development process, or you ignore them and test your product some other way (such as with manual testing). I've experienced software projects without unit tests, and I've been scared enough to consider unit testing a mandatory practice for every project I work on.

Imagine starting a new job as a software developer, and on day one you're asked to change a considerable portion of the codebase because the previous developers hardcoded a set of configuration parameters. These parameters now need to be extracted from a centralized secrets vault (a third-party API that you query via HTTP). In theory, the task is not too complex; you need to find the right place to perform the request, and then you need to pass the newly retrieved properties everywhere they were being used before.

This could be as easy and as painless as modifying a few lines of code and adding a few more for your request. Or it could be as painful and complicated as having to rewrite a whole section of the codebase because those properties were taken from global variables, and there is no way to inject any dependencies. Either way, the question then is, how can you be sure after you've made all those changes that everything still works as expected?

That, my dear reader and fellow software developer, is why we unit test. Not because we need to get to know a codebase, or because we don't know any better, but rather because we need to understand how stable our code is. Once you (or someone else) make changes to your code, will it keep working as intended? That is how you measure code stability. Think of the unit test as a snapshot of the intended functionality of a piece of code and running the tests as comparing the old snapshot to the current picture. Are they still the same? If so, the change didn't break anything. If they're different, something's wrong. Either the test is no longer valid and needs to be updated, or the change introduced unwanted errors. Unit tests are far from basic, and considering them a task for a junior developer shows that you don't really know what they are or why you should be using them.

Unit tests are the safety net of software development, if you use them properly, that is. But like with any safety net, just having the net doesn't make it safe. If you don't follow the proper safety measures, and you set it up too low, the result when you fall will be exactly the same as if you didn't have it in the first place: you'll hit the ground and turn into mashed potato. I don't mean to scare you, but working on a project without unit tests is like walking on a tightrope without a safety net under you and with a bunch of hungry crocodiles waiting at the bottom of the pit, with laser eyes and iron spikes on their tails. That metaphor grew out of proportion, but you get the point: you should indeed be scared.

Unit tests are there to provide future safety. And by *future*, I mean any point in time beyond today. You (or someone else) could come back to this code tomorrow or in five years, and as long as the tests are there to ensure that the logical contract is solid, any and all changes you perform on that code will be checked for consistency.

3.1.1 *What about using unit tests today?*

Unit tests are also a great tool for today, thanks to a practice that almost nobody uses daily, called *test-driven development* (TDD). TDD is a way of writing code that involves writing the unit tests first and the code later. TDD is great on paper. The only problem with it, and the main reason we're not all using it daily and for every project we work on, is that it changes the way developers work so much that not all of us are willing to adjust.

Normal development works like this: When you see a problem and decide to write code to fix it, the first thing you do is create a quick mental model of the solution— the good old "to solve *C*, I need to provide *B*, which I get through *A*, so it's all about getting *A* then *B* and finally *C*." Then you turn that into code. You can't help it, you're a developer and that's how your mind works.

TDD is different in that it helps ensure that common bugs are never introduced into our code by making sure you test the code and every edge case around it first. Tests drive the development, instead of having the developed code drive the tests we create around it. This shift in our mindset is what prevents most developers from adopting TDD. After all, it's hard to change the way we're wired to think about problems.

The normal workflow of a TDD-based project is represented in figure 3.1.

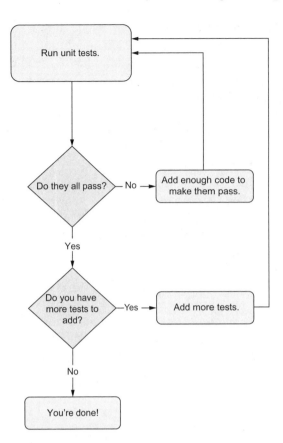

Figure 3.1 Decision tree when performing TDD

Figure 3.1 shows how simple the workflow is when working with TDD:

1 Create the tests for feature *A*.
2 Run the tests.
3 Check the test results:
   - If they failed, write some code and go back to step 2.
   - If they passed, move on to the next feature.

The problem with TDD is that when we're just getting started, creating tests against code that hasn't yet been written sounds scary. How can you test feature *A* when it hasn't been written yet?

Let's look at a basic example. Suppose you're working on a JavaScript math library and you're coding the division operation. "Not that big of a deal," you think. "I can write a test for it in 10 minutes," and you write the following code.

Listing 3.1 Simple unit test for the division method

```
const mathlib = require("./index")
const assert = require('assert');
```

```
describe("My Math library, division operator", () => {
    it("should correctly divide two numbers", () => {
        let result = mathlib.division(2, 2)
        assert.equal(result, 1)        <──── The test itself
    })
})
```

The test is simple enough. You call the operation and make sure the result is valid. That, in turn, will lead you to write a version of the method like the following.

Listing 3.2 First version of the division method that passes the test in listing 3.1

```
exports.division = (a, b) => {
    return a / b;
}
```

It seems correct, doesn't it? Well, if you were properly performing TDD, you would ask yourself, "How can I break this function?" Right off the top of my head, I can think of two easy ways:

- You can pass 0 as the second parameter.
- You can pass something that's not a number as any of the parameters.

Can you think of any other way of breaking the method? TDD is not just about testing the basics but rather about going deep into every single use case. Collect all the answers you came up with, and create a test for each one of them (that's right, create tests, not code yet). The following listing shows the two new tests I created.

Listing 3.3 Updated test suite

```
describe("My Math library, division operator", () => {
    it("should correctly divide two numbers", () => {  <──── The basic test
        console.log(mathlib)
        let result = mathlib.division(2, 2)
        assert.equal(result, 1)
    })
    it("should not allow receiving a 0 as the second parameter", () => {
        assert.throws(() => {
            let result = mathlib.division(2, 0)  <──── Checking for division by 0
        }, /Division by 0 not allowed/)
    })
    it("should not allow receiving non-numeric attributes", () => {
        assert.throws(() => {
            let result = mathlib.division("23", [2,4])  <──── Checking for invalid types
        }, /Non-numeric parameters received/)
    })
})
```

The updated test suite with the division by zero and the check for invalid types covers our simple division method in more detail and with our business logic in mind. The next listing shows what the second version of our method would look like.

Listing 3.4   Updated division method

```
exports.division = (a, b) => {
    if(b == 0) {                                        ◁─── Checking for division by 0
        throw new Error('Division by 0 not allowed')
    }
    //Parse into numbers in case they're types that can be cast into number
    a = +a;
    b = +b;
    if(isNaN(a) || isNaN(b)) {         ◁───┐  Checking for non-numeric values
        throw new Error('Non-numeric parameters received')
    }
    return a / b;
}
```

Now our simple method looks a lot more complex. You've now removed the possibility of basic bugs, thanks to this new way of coding. TDD is fantastic, and it looks great on paper, but getting everyone on your team to adapt to it might not be easy.

This is what you did by using TDD: you built your tests assuming the code existed (even though it didn't at first). You imported a file that didn't exist, assuming it exported a function that hadn't been created yet, and you used it with a signature that hadn't been defined. Did it fail? Yes! It failed on your first try because the file you were importing didn't exist. You then created it and went back to step 1. It failed again because the file was empty, so you wrote an empty function and exported it. It failed again because the function was empty. You then filled up the function with code that made all the tests pass.

TDD is not just about testing the basics but rather about going deep into every single use case. Unit tests are important, and they're very useful in ensuring that your code works now and in the future after you change it. However, there is a lot more to tests than just the basic validations in listing 3.3. The first question you have to answer is, "What will I test?" Not all code is meant to be tested.

3.2   What to test

Writing code without tests is dangerous and ill advised. However, the other extreme of writing "all the tests" is just as bad. You'd be wasting a lot of time testing code that doesn't have to be tested. You have to learn to identify what to test and what to ignore. Remember, there is code that is not meant to be tested, and there are interactions that are not meant to be let loose and uncontrolled (in other words, not tested, hoping that they work as expected).

Consider the following very common scenario. You're assigned to create tests for a system that, among other things, gathers data from some third-party APIs and saves it to a database. You need to test the code involved in those interactions.

Several questions are likely to come to mind. How do you test those interactions? Are you going to send requests to those APIs? What about the results? Are you going to save those to the database, or maybe to a testing database? What do you do with the data once you're done? These are all very valid (yet wrong) questions to ask yourself, and we've all been there. You're focusing on the interactions instead of asking more basic questions still, such as "What should I be testing?"

Let's look at what you should actually consider when starting your testing task.

3.2.1 Test one thing at the time

The first thing to remember is that each test should test one thing, and one thing only. It can be tempting to add multiple checks into a single test, especially if they're related, but suppose one of those tests fails. Suddenly you have multiple checks associated with the same error message. Ideally, you want one check per test so that when things go wrong, you have the information to understand where the error lies.

Imagine the checks in listing 3.3 all being inside the same test (the first one). If one of them were to fail, you'd get an error saying something like "My Math library, division operator—It should correctly divide two numbers." How is that useful? I'll answer that for you: it's not.

As a rule of thumb, every unit test should only have one `assert` or `expect` (or equivalent statement for the language and framework combination you're using). The error message associated with the test should also be very informative. A message like "It should correctly divide two numbers" is not good enough. Write clear and unambiguous expectations like, "It should support the second parameter being 0." If you find yourself writing a vague error message, that might be a sign that you're not testing the right thing. If the message is specific enough, that will help make your test specific enough.

3.2.2 Make sure you test a unit of code

Another common question we have when starting to write tests is which parts of the code need to be tested. We could easily assume the right answer would be "all of it," but it's not. Unit tests are named that because they test a *unit* of code. That's a very vague definition, but you can think of a unit as an atomic piece of logic that is complex enough to be tested. By *atomic* I mean that you can't split it up without losing part of it's intended logic.

Consider the following code, where we have a function with multiple scenarios inside.

Listing 3.5 How many tests would you write for this function?

```
function mergeLists(listA, listB) {       Not testable—simple assignment
    let result = []               <———

    if(!Array.isArray(listA)) {       <——— Scenario 1
        throw new Error("First parameter must be an array")
    }
    if(!Array.isArray(listB)) {       <——— Scenario 2
        throw new Error("Second parameter must be an array")
    }
    result = [...listA, ...listB]     <——— Not testable—merging two arrays
```

```
console.log("Debug: total items: ", result.length)
return result
}
```

Scenario 3 ← `return result`

Not testable—
simple console.log ← `console.log("Debug: total items: ", result.length)`

How many tests would you write for this function? A single test wouldn't cover the whole thing, at least not following the standards we're discussing here. You can't write a single test to check scenarios 1–3. They're very distinct logic paths that don't overlap. Instead, the right thing to do would be to test each of the three individually.

However, notice that there are some lines we're ignoring. They're either too simple to be tested (for instance, a simple variable assignment or a console.log line) or their logic is captured by some of the scenarios we'll be tackling in our tests (like the merging of two arrays).

Here's a good guideline when it comes to picking which parts of the code to test:

- You'll want to write one test for the main logic path (to check exactly what the function or method you're testing is meant to be doing). In this case, that would be scenario 3, which covers the final result of the function.
- Then you'll want to write one test for every logic path that diverges from the main one. In this example, that would be scenarios 1 and 2, which return prematurely if any of the attributes aren't valid arrays.

With this approach, you won't have any problems coming up with test cases for more complex and longer functions. Just break them up into logic paths, and you'll be fine.

3.2.3 *Only test your own code*

Try to avoid writing tests that include logic from third-party libraries. In our industry, the phrase "Don't reinvent the wheel" is a mantra we all live by—so much so that there are millions (I'm not exaggerating) of open source libraries ready for you for whatever you're trying to accomplish. There are database drivers, MVC frameworks, HTTP communication libraries, and many others that give you the tools to perform everyday tasks. They let you build things using other people's blocks.

How is this relevant to our testing? When you write your tests, don't waste any time writing testing logic from these third-party blocks. They should already have been tested by their authors. "But what if they haven't?" you ask. Then don't use them. Luckily for us, not everyone listens to "Don't reinvent the wheel," so there's not just one library for every use case. In fact, you have multiple ways of solving the same problem, thanks to the multitude of similar, yet slightly different, open source projects. Just make sure that the one you pick is properly tested.

How can you tell if a library or framework has a test suite? Well, if it's an open source project (which they usually are), you will probably have access to their code and can check for the files containing the unit tests. Sometimes the documentation shows you how to run the tests, which implies the tests are there. Finally, if it's a closed-source solution, it's safe to assume the tests are there. Ultimately, if you have doubts about whether there are tests, and an alternative that is clearly tested exists, go for that one.

By using third-party tested code, you don't need to worry about testing it yourself. For instance, a common scenario would be to test a function like the following.

Listing 3.6 Testing only your own code

```
function saveUser(userObj, mysqLDB) {
    if(!userObj) {
        throw new Error("Missing userObj, please send a valid object")
    }
    if(!validateUsrData(userObj)) {               <──── Test!
        throw new Error("User data is not valid")
    }


    return mysqLDB.query(`Insert into Users (username, address,   <──── Ignore!
                          first_name, last_name) values `,
                          ["(", userObj.username, userObj.address,
                          userObj.fname, userObj.lname, ")"].join(","))
}
```

Test! ▭──▷ (marker pointing at `if(!userObj) {`)

Out of the three scenarios in listing 3.6, you should only care about the first two, which cover logic paths you had to write yourself. The third should be ignored because it directly uses the MySQL driver that you pass as a parameter. That driver wasn't written by you, so the main focus of your tests shouldn't be whether or not the data gets saved to the database (that is covered by the tests for the `query` method). Instead, your tests should focus on what happens when the `userObj` object is not valid.

3.2.4 *Don't test external calls*

Just as you shouldn't bother testing code and logic from third-party libraries, you should also prevent them from making external calls because unit tests are meant to be run in isolation. An external call can be almost anything: it can be a query to the database, a connection request, an HTTP request to an external API, or a file read request to the OS. Anything that breaks the bubble of your code should be contained.

Remember how I said you should be focusing on testing a "unit" of code? Well, that unit can't be affected by its environment; otherwise, you're no longer testing a unit of logic, but rather the environment's effect on it. It's a subtle difference, but consider what would happen if we were to test the code from listing 3.6. We would need at least three scenarios:

- Test with an empty `userObj` object to ensure that the first `if` statement checks for a valid object.
- Test with an invalid `userObj` object to check the second scenario, which is the result of validating the structure of the data received.
- Test with a valid `userObj` object to check that the previous scenarios are not triggering with a valid object.

The problem with the last test is that our code will be fully executed, and the testing user will be saved to the database. Not only that, but our test would now be entirely dependent on the status of the database connection. That's the environment affecting our test. If the database connection closes during the test (perhaps because the database is undergoing maintenance), our tests would fail, but it would not be due to a problem with our logic. We would no longer be testing our logic but the environment's effect on it. That is incorrect, at least for a unit test.

Solving this problem can be as easy as using dependency injection or as complex as using dependency injection. You didn't read that wrong—the solution to our problem is dependency injection (DI), but if the tested code is not written to support DI, applying it can be really hard.

In a nutshell, dependency injection allows you to overwrite external dependencies using other libraries. In this example, for unit tests, you'd inject a dependency that is under your control and does exactly what you need to ensure the logic flow inside your test. In some instances, you may need to refactor the tested code to allow for DI, and in other situations, you may need to go meta and override some of the language's core mechanics.

> **NOTE**   *Metaprogramming* is the practice of changing the language's default behavior to achieve what you want.

Dependency injection is one of the best tools you can have at your disposal when testing code that interacts (directly or indirectly) with external resources. Don't worry if it sounds too complex right now. I'll cover it more in detail in section 3.3.1, so soon it'll all make sense.

3.2.5   *Stick to testing what's on the rug*

Finally, when it comes to picking which parts of your code to test, another good rule of thumbs is to only test what other people see. Many programming languages allow you to hide code so it can't be accessed, such as private properties and methods for some OOP languages (such as Java or C#) and functions that aren't exported from modules in languages such as JavaScript. So what should your tests focus on?

Your unit tests should only test what the users of your code (other developers) will get to see and use. Why? Because chances are your private code will be indirectly tested by you when you test the public-facing portion of your code. Also, there is no easy way for you to test private code without making it public, so you would end up breaking the encapsulation of your code only to test it.

In listing 3.6 we had a function called `saveUser`. Imagine seeing the overall context of that function, as in the following listing.

Listing 3.7   Full context of the function from listing 3.6

```
/**
 * Validates that the user object to be saved into the database
 * has all the required attributes.
```

```
 *
 * @param {User} userObj
 * @returns TRUE if it does, FALSE otherwise.
 */
function validateUsrData(userObj) {      ⟵—— This function is not exported.
    if(!userObj.username) return false
    if(!userObj.address) return false
    if(!userObj.fname) return false
    if(!userObj.lname) return false

    return true
}


export function saveUser(
    userObj,
    mysqLDB                          This function is exported
                                     out of the module.
) {
    //... some of the function's code goes here     We're calling a private
    if(!validateUsrData(userObj)) {                 function here.
        throw new Error("User data is not valid")
    }
    //... the rest of the function's code
}
```

I've trimmed the content of the saveUser function a bit in listing 3.7 because we don't need to look at it again in detail. However, with the full context, we can see three things:

- This is a JavaScript module.
- The module is exporting one (only one) function: saveUser.
- The validateUsrData function is not exported out of the module, so it's considered private.

Now it makes sense that your tests should focus on saveUser. The code from validate-UsrData will still be tested, only indirectly by our tests.

You should now have a good understanding of what to start testing. But if you haven't done testing before, you might not know *how* to do it. Let's take a look at some best practices for writing your tests.

3.3   *How to write your tests*

Let's pretend that you're starting a new job and joining an already established project. This means there is a lot of base code to understand and read. To help you in that task, your team lead assigns you to create some pending unit tests. This will be a great opportunity for you to understand the code and how it works. At least in theory.

A lot of questions are triggered in the back of your head. What do you do first? Or better yet, what should you look for in that code? What tools do you have at your disposal? How can you overwrite those external dependencies we talked about? These are great questions; let's dive into the answers.

3.3.1 *Your new best friend: Dependency injection*

It's time to look at dependency injection. I've already mentioned it, but it's time we get familiar with it. Dependency injection essentially means that instead of handling external dependencies (third-party libraries and external resources) as global variables, we handle them as received parameters.

In other words, if you are writing a class that wraps around another library, make sure you receive the library (or an instance of it) as a parameter on the constructor. If you are writing a common module, accept its dependencies as attributes when importing it. If you do this, you can easily overwrite these external libraries and files with the ones you want, which comes in very handy when you're writing tests. Why is that? As I already mentioned, external dependencies are a big no-no when writing and executing unit tests. When you write a test, you need to be in control of every single aspect of its context.

Suppose we're testing a piece of code that extracts a list of countries from an external API and returns the ones that start with a particular letter. If you don't control what the API returns, how can you be sure the code of your tests will even make sense?

Listing 3.8 Tests that are are entirely dependent on external results

```
describe("API Wrapper class", () => {
    it("getTop5Countries should list the first 5 countries "+
       "starting with the given letter", () => {
        const wrapper = new MyWrapper('A')
        const results = wrapper.getTop5Countries()          ◁─── Call to external API
        assert.strictEqual(result, ['Afghanistan', 'Albania',
                                    'Algeria', 'Andorra', 'Angola'])
    })
})
```

Listing 3.8 shows where the dependency with the external API is, and you can probably guess that this is not ideal. What if the call to getTop5Countries fails because the API is down? Our test will fail even when our code is correct because we're not just testing our code, we're testing the connectivity with the API.

Consider now adding a quick check to validate if the API is up and working before you send the actual request. You can't control when that happens, so how can you write such a test? Notice that we're not testing the connectivity here either, but rather the code we added to handle that scenario.

We need to find a way to eliminate the dependency on the external API and gain full control over what we receive from it and how it behaves. That way, we can control scenarios like error responses, lack of data, lack of communication, and so on. This is where dependency injection comes into play. The very simple change in the following listing makes everything easier.

Listing 3.9 Allowing for dependency injection

```
it("getTop5Countries should list the first 5 countries "+
   "starting with the given letter", () => {
   const wrapper = new MyWrapper('A', requestLibrary)

   const results = wrapper.getTop5Countries()
   assert.strictEqual(result, ['Afghanistan', 'Albania', 'Algeria',
                               'Andorra', 'Angola'])
})
```

Passing requestLibrary as a parameter

Here, accepting a second parameter on the constructor of the class allows us to pass a fake request library that, instead of sending an HTTP request to the real API, doesn't do anything. Or, even better, it can do what we want it to do.

Let's take a closer look at what we can do with this fake request library. In the following listing, we'll assume that the `makeRequest` method is the one our wrapper class calls when using the request library.

Listing 3.10 Controlling the behavior of the API

```
it("getTop5Countries should list the first 5 countries " +
   "starting with the given letter", () => {
   const requestLibrary = {
     makeRequest: () => {
       return ['Afghanistan', 'Albania', 'Algeria', 'Andorra', 'Angola']
     }
   }
   const wrapper = new MyWrapper('A', requestLibrary)
   const results = wrapper.getTop5Countries()
   assert.strictEqual(result, ['Afghanistan', 'Albania', 'Algeria',
                               'Andorra', 'Angola'])
})

it("getTop5Countries should return an empty list if " +
   "there are no countries with that letter", () => {
   const requestLibrary = {
     makeRequest: () => false
   }
   const wrapper = new MyWrapper('A', requestLibrary)

   const results = wrapper.getTop5Countries()
   assert.strictEqual(result, [])
})

it("getTop5Countries should throw an error if the API is "+
   "not reachable", () => {
   const requestLibrary = {
     makeRequest: () => {
       throw new Error("Unable to access the API")
     }
   }
   const wrapper = new MyWrapper('A', requestLibrary)
```

Scenario 1, everything working fine

Scenario 2, no data from API

Scenario 3, can't reach the API

```
    assert.throws(() => {
      wrapper.getTop5Countries()
    })
  }, /Unable to access the API/)
```

This is a very naive representation, but you'll base all your tests on this basic principle. You'll have to reimplement some of the key methods to control the behavior of the API. By doing so, you can test how your code responds to specific scenarios instead of testing how the API behaves. For example, scenario 1 shows how we would ensure the "happy path," by returning what we'd expect the API to return. In scenarios 2 and 3, we're forcing the empty response (in the second scenario) and a thrown exception (in the third and final scenario) to verify how our code handles those scenarios.

This has been a brief introduction to dependency injection, but you should be able to see why you'd want to use it often. Let's now take a closer look at other tools you can use in conjunction with DI to get the most out of it.

3.3.2   *Tame the big four: Mocks, stubs, spies, and dummies*

Mastering these four concepts—mocks, stubs, spies, and dummies—will make you a unit-testing superhero. If you don't learn about these, you'll spend most of your time coming up with workarounds, trying to emulate them without even knowing it. These concepts will all help you, but with slightly different features or ways of using them, so it's important to understand all four.

The idea behind all four is essentially that of the fake request library we used in listing 3.10. In that example, we created a custom object with a particular method (the one we were using in our main code), but that's a short-term solution that works in some languages, such as JavaScript, but not in others. With mocks, stubs, spies, and dummies, you'll be able to not only emulate a dependency's behavior (such as our request library in the previous example) but also get a lot more information about what happens when your tests execute your code.

In the following discussion, keep in mind that every language has its own testing frameworks, and each has its own way of implementing these concepts. I won't focus on specific code here but rather on concepts. Once you understand the concepts, you can look up how to implement them in your framework or language of choice. I promise you, there is already a library or framework waiting for you.

STUBBING YOUR WAY THROUGH TESTS

You've seen one stub already. The fake request library object we created is formally known as a *stub*. Essentially, stubbing is about creating a fake version of an object, or a function inside a module, or even a method inside an object. This fully fake version of the code will do exactly what you need to ensure the logic path you want to test.

You'll normally want to stub key blocks of code that help determine a particular logic path, such as code that queries an external service, like we did before. This allows you to test for valid results, empty results, invalid results, problems with the connection, and everything in between.

You can also stub whatever else you want, such as an internal validation function. Imagine you're testing the logic around an endpoint handler on your REST API. Your code is supposed to receive a request, validate it, and then decide whether to format the object and save it to the database or to return an error. You could attempt to test that logic by passing in different requests—a valid one when you want to test for the happy path or an invalid one when you want to check the error path. However, that approach couples the test's logic with the implementation of the validation function.

Consider what would happen if tomorrow you added an extra required attribute to the request. Suddenly some of your tests would fail because the tests that were sending valid requests are no longer doing so. However, your handler code (and its required logic) is still intact. What changed was the validation function (which would have been tested somewhere else).

This is where a stub for an internal function comes in very handy. You can overwrite that validation with a stub and control exactly what happens on every test. If tomorrow the requirement changes again, you'll probably need another test to pick that change up, but this one will still be correct.

MOCKS, STUB'S DISTANT COUSIN

Mocks are another useful tool to have in your unit-testing belt. They're very similar to stubs—so much so that many developers confuse them with each other. The key difference is that instead of overwriting the original logic (stub), you wrap it (mock), allowing you to then verify what happened to it (Was it called? Did it receive parameters? What parameters was it called with? And so on.). You can also preset the expected behavior of a mock so that when it's executed, the mocked function or method will return what you want.

When creating a mock, you pick a function or method and set expectations for it. This essentially means you tell it that you expect the function to be called with a particular set of parameters, and when that happens, you expect it to return something in particular. However, the original code remains the same.

Mocks are great tools for verifying interactions between components of your logic. For example, let's consider a validation function that checks for the attributes received in a handler function. If you stub it, you can't really tell if the function is receiving the right parameters—you're just checking what happens when it returns success or failure. By mocking it, you could validate the interaction our code has with it.

We could mock the validation function, which essentially means you call a special function that wraps the original validation function and yields a mock object (the wrapped function, which contains extra logic required by the mock). We could then set the expectations for that object, such as specifying that the function should be called only once with a predefined list of parameters, and when that happens it should return `true`.

We could then proceed to write the rest of the test, which would call our handler function (not the validation function) and then ask the mock object to verify its status. The following listing shows some pseudocode that illustrates this without going deep into any language.

Listing 3.11   Pseudocode showing how a mock works

```
test("it should fail with error 400 when the username is missing") {
  var validationMock = new Mock(validationsObject)       ◁─────┐ We create the mock here.
  validationMock.expect("validateUser")
          .calledWith(['address', 'first_name', 'last_name'])
          .toReturn({ "error": "Missing username", statusCode: 400})
  var fakeRequest = {
      "address": "My street 999, My City",
      "first_name": "Fernando",
      "last_name": "Doglio"
  }
  var result = endpointHandler(fakeRequest, validationsObject)
  validationMock.verify()            ◁─────┐ We verify the behavior here.
  expect(result.statusCode).toBe(400)
}
```

We set expectations here.

There are a few things to note in listing 3.11:

- We're taking advantage of dependency injection to create the mock because we have access to the `validationsObject` library. If this was handled directly inside our handler code as a global variable, we would be out of luck.
- The first thing we do is create the mock object, wrapping the entire `validationsObject` entity.
- We set the expectations on the mock, but we leave the original object alone. We tell it to expect its `validateUser` method to be called with three parameters (instead of the four we know it needs), and we tell it that we expect it to return JSON with the right error message for that situation.
- At the end of the test, we check to make sure that both expectations were met. Note that this check is sometimes done implicitly by the framework, in which case there is no need for you to worry about it.

With a mock, we can solve the issue we mentioned during our discussion of stubs. If tomorrow we add a new required parameter, the expectations we set for our mock will fail because the error message will probably not be the same (it should mention the missing new parameter).

Mocks are fake objects with predefined behavior (like stubs) and expectations. They do not do what you want, but they make sure you're using the mocked code as expected. If these expectations aren't met, your test will fail.

SPYING ON YOUR CODE

If you want to take expectations to the next level, you can leave mocks behind and start using *spies*. These are wrappers around your code, just like mocks, but spies record everything that happens to them. Instead of setting expectations and waiting to see if they're met, you can simply execute your code and spy on it to check how your code was executed. As with mocks, you can use spies to understand how your code interacts with other functions, how often, and with what parameters.

We can rewrite listing 3.11 to use spies, and the intention of the test would remain the same. The following listing shows what that rewrite might look like.

Listing 3.12 Testing our code using spies

```
test("it should fail with error 400 when the username is missing") {
  var spiedMethod = new Spy(validationsObject, "validateUser")   ◁──┐ We spy one
                                                                     │ method.
  var fakeRequest = {
      "address": "My street 999, My City",
      "first_name": "Fernando",
      "last_name": "Doglio"
  }

  var result = endpointHanlder(fakeRequest, validationsObject)

  expect(spiedMethod)                          ◁──────────┐ We check what happened
    .toHaveBeenCalled                                     │ to our spied method.
    .with(['address', 'first_name', 'last_name'])
    .toReturn({"error": "Missing username attribute", statusCode: 400})

  expect(result.statusCode).toBe(400)
}
```

Listing 3.12 is again in pseudocode to avoid getting into the specifics of any particular framework or language. However, you can see that we're asking the spy what happened with the method. We first set up the spy on a single method, we execute our code, and at the end, as part of the checks performed, we validate the recorded information.

Depending on the framework or library you're using, you might have access to the number of times the method was called, all the parameters received on every call, the result, and more. Read the documentation before assuming anything.

YOU DUMMY!

Finally, we have dummies. These are simply empty methods created to ensure the code works. Depending on the language you are using, they may or may not be useful. In loosely typed languages such as JavaScript or Python, you can create objects and functions without much fuss. However, some other languages, mainly strongly typed languages, require you to be very specific about the types of objects you use and the number of parameters you pass to your functions. Dummies can help you meet these requirements.

The following listing shows a quick test using Deno with TypeScript (I'm using a particular language here because dummies aren't useful in all languages).

Listing 3.13 Using dummies in Deno with TypeScript

```
Deno.test("Request handler throws an exception if header 'Auth' " +
          "is not present", () => {
    const handler = new MyAPI()          ┌ This is a dummy
    const resp: HTTPResponse = {    ◁─────┘ response object.
```

```
        send: (txt: string) => {
        }
    }
    assertThrows( () => {
        handler.requestHandler({body:'', headers: []} as HTTPRequest, resp)
    }, Error, "Missing Auth header")
});
```

Here we create the `resp` object with an empty `send` method. That's a dummy right there. The method is never called because the `requestHandler` method will throw an exception before it gets to calling the method. But we need the method because TypeScript will force us to comply with the signature of the `requestHandler` method.

WHEN DO YOU USE WHAT?

Stubs, mocks, spies, and dummies can be confusing. In some situations, the boundaries between them can get blurry, so it's important to understand when it's best to use each one. Unfortunately, there is no clear formula to follow in most cases, so I recommend going for the simplest solution.

Stubs can used instead of mocks if you want, and spies can replace mocks and stubs and add more behavior. I recommend developers choose this way:

- Do you need to overwrite a function or a method from a dependency to ensure the logic flow of your test? Then stubs it is.
- Do you also need to understand how methods are being called? Do you need to test that your code is calling functions with particular parameters? Then mocks are probably what you need.
- Perhaps you want even more details about which functions are being called and the parameters being used for those calls. That is where spies come into play, giving you ultimate control over what your code is doing and how it is doing it.

Dummies, in contrast, are quite straightforward. They're empty objects or functions that are needed to satisfy a particular interface. You can use them in conjunction with mocks, stubs, or spies when you overwrite a function call and don't need all the parameters.

With experience, you'll start preferring one approach over the other, and that's okay. But if you're just getting started, follow the preceding recommendations, and you'll be fine.

3.3.3   *Unit tests are not meant to be run manually*

As a small corollary to everything we've been discussing so far, you need to understand that unit tests aren't intended to be a manual tool that you can execute whenever you want. Unit tests are meant to ensure that everything works after you or someone else has made a change, now or in the future. That check needs to happen often, and it can't be dependent on whether or not you remember to do it.

As part of the development process, the running of tests has to be automated. I won't cover this automation, since each tool has its own configuration and associated workflows. If you're working with web technologies, it would be a good idea to read about bundlers. If you're dealing with a continuous integration (CI) or continuous delivery (CD) platform such as Jenkins (www.jenkins.io), Travis CI (https://travis-ci.org), or others, their documentation should have the required information.

Setting up an automation to run the unit tests right before you commit your code is a great idea. That way, you ensure no failing tests are sent to the repository.

If you're building a large enough system, automating the execution of all tests during the CI phase might be a great alternative. That way, you can deploy the entire application and execute all the unit tests individually on a large server (so you don't have to tax your local development machine).

Yet another place to execute the tests could be right before the merge of pull requests on GitHub. Thanks to GitHub actions, which are essentially scripts that are executed based on different triggers, you can automate the execution of the tests and cancel the merging process if they don't succeed. This allows you to keep your main branches clean of dirty code (code that hasn't been fully tested or even finished).

Whichever approach you choose, developers shouldn't be in charge of remembering when to run these tests. The tests should happen as one of the many automated processes in your project. Most importantly, a negative result needs to cancel the process until the tests are fixed.

With that said, there is one more thing you need to know about unit tests before we can move on to the next chapter: when exactly should you write your tests? I've already hinted at it, but let's get into the details.

3.4 When should you write your tests?

There are two times when you have to remember to write unit tests for your code: during the development of a feature and when you change the code of a feature.

There is no better time to write tests and test your code than during the development of a feature. If you want to get into TDD and write the tests before the actual feature code, even better. Thinking that your code covers every edge case without writing tests to prove that is naive at best. Without careful testing, you can't be sure.

The process of developing a feature is a bit like a walk in the park. You can focus on the destination and dive head first into coding the feature—this approach will get you to the finishing line faster, but you'll miss a lot of interesting details on the way. You'll then have to write the tests later, based on what you remember of your walk. Alternatively, you can tackle it by thinking about and enjoying the walk and your surroundings, and you'll be more open to discovering interesting edge cases along the way. This approach lets you create more detailed and meaningful tests because you're still in the middle of designing the business logic.

When you are planning a feature your team is going to work on, you need to factor in the time that it will take to write the tests into your schedule. If you don't, you'll be underestimating the effort required. As a good rule of thumb, add 15% more time to dedicate to tests. Of course, if you have a better metric based on your own experience, you should use that.

The other time when you'll want to work with unit tests is during code changes. You need to make sure that your tests reflect any changes you make, be it a refactoring due to technical debt, a bug fix, or whatever other reason was behind the change. This is easy to do if the tests fail when you change the code, but you'll only know that if you're automatically running the tests, as I suggested earlier. If you don't have automated tests, you might run into the classic trap of thinking you're making a small enough change that it won't affect anything, when, in reality, you're breaking tests, but you just don't know it yet.

If you make changes to existing code, especially code that you didn't write, you'll usually break the tests around it. If I change more than one line I didn't write and the tests don't fail, I tend to think that either the tests are not correctly testing the code, or I've added a logical path that was never considered in the tests. Whether you're updating code, adding a bug fix, or refactoring bad code, remember to have an automated test process to make sure your changes haven't affected anything you're not directly seeing.

Summary

- Writing unit tests isn't just a task for junior developers as they get to know the codebase. Instead, they're the perfect tool to make sure your code works as expected now and in the future.
- You should only test your own code—third-party libraries should have already been tested by their own authors. External resources must be mocked, or you'll be coupling the logic of your tests with the ability to reach those external services.
- You can use dependency injection to overwrite an external dependency, removing the uncertainty it added.
- You can use stubs to overwrite methods or functions to suit the needs of your tests without affecting the original code.
- Mocks can do what stubs do, but they also let you add expectations, helping you test how functions interact with each other.
- Spies can give you even more control than mocks, with an API you can query to determine things like the number of calls to a function and the list of parameters received.
- Dummies can help you fill in the blanks when you use stubs and mocks with unused or inaccessible parameters.

Refactoring existing code (or Refactoring doesn't mean rewriting code)

This chapter covers

- How to plan a refactor and what to consider while doing so
- What to look for while refactoring code
- Tools and techniques you can use to refactor code
- Where refactoring code does not make any sense

Aside from unit testing, the importance of refactoring and the correct way of doing it is one of the most valuable things you can learn early in your career as a software developer. If you want to properly refactor your or other people's code, you'll have to learn all you can about best coding practices, and you'll have to be able to pick up on anti-patterns that need to be broken down, rearranged, and cleaned up.

Ironically, doing a proper refactoring of a codebase requires years of experience, which you probably don't have yet. So why am I bothering to talk about it? Because you can't get experience doing proper code refactors if you don't know what a proper code refactor involves. You need to understand what to look for and what you should do when you find something that needs to be reworked.

It's that simple. This chapter won't make you an expert on the subject, but it'll give you a glimpse of what you have yet to learn. I'll cover the basics—everything you need to understand about refactoring, and the tools that senior developers use when they read and refactor code. The rest will come once you start doing it over and over.

4.1   *What does refactoring mean anyway?*

The first thing you need to understand is exactly what refactoring entails. To the untrained eye, refactoring might just seem to be "rewriting existing code," but there is a lot more to it than that. In fact, I would define it as "restructuring existing logic," because that includes not only changing code around but also splitting up sections of your business logic into multiple modules, reworking how the data flows from point A to B, or even simply changing it so that it is easier for others to understand.

Granted, you can't do what I just described without rewriting existing code, but just rewriting code is not refactoring. Rewriting is the most basic tool you'll use when refactoring.

You'll want to refactor your code for various reasons:

- Sometimes fixing a bug requires refactoring because the bug is due to incorrectly constructed logic. This might result in you having to rearrange your code, extract part of your logic, and change the way it is used. All those major changes can be considered a refactoring.

- Sometimes you'll want to change a piece of code to make it more generic and reusable by others, such as to turn a section of your logic into a generic library. That's a major refactoring and a great use of this technique.

- Sometimes refactoring is just about cleaning up the code so it's easier to read, without affecting the logic (in other words, moving things around). For example, when new developers start using classes, they sometimes create big files with several classes all jammed in together. That code will work without a problem, but it'll be harder to read, maintain, and understand because it's hard for humans to search through and read thousands of lines of code inside a file. But if you do a simple refactoring and move each class into its own file, you'll end up with very specific files that are each smaller and easier to understand. The code is exactly the same; all that was done was a simple refactoring, but the benefit is major. Of course, no matter how good your refactoring is in this scenario, there is no substitute for proper documentation.

I can hear you thinking, "But isn't all of that just rewriting existing code?" Yes, we're changing code, but conceptually we're dealing with higher-level entities such as classes, logic paths, and readability. Focusing just on the action of changing code trivializes the different techniques and concepts you'll see in this chapter. The reason there is a whole practice around changing code is that when you do it with purpose, it takes on a whole different meaning.

Let's now take a quick look at what you'll want to look for when you're thinking about refactoring a piece of code. If you still have any doubts, they'll be cleared up once we start applying these concepts.

4.2 *What do you do before you start refactoring?*

Before you even start to think about moving code around, you need to understand the prior steps that need to be taken. To paraphrase Boromir from *The Lord of the Rings*, "One does not simply start moving code around without a safety net."[1] And in Boromir's defense, while you *could* do so, if you skip the safety net, you won't be able to undo your work when something goes wrong.

Suppose you've been working for a while on a project, and a section of your code is so well structured and useful that your tech lead requests that you turn it into an independent library, so other teams in the company can use it.

"That's fantastic," you immediately think. "I'll start chopping at the code right away," you answer.

"Just make sure your original code is not affected by that," answers your tech lead, with the wisdom gained from years of experience.

You're immediately frozen in place. You thought this was going to be as easy as creating a new project with your code inside it, but now you have to somehow ensure that your project isn't affected. What do you do first?

This is not an uncommon scenario. In fact, with time you'll start suggesting these changes yourself to your tech lead. After all, generalizing logic and abstracting patterns away is something that developers do very well in all aspects of life. Have you ever heard this joke:

> My wife said, "Go to the store and buy a carton of milk, and if they have eggs, get a dozen."
> I came back with 12 cartons of milk. She said, "Why in the heck did you buy twelve cartons of milk?" "They had eggs," I replied.

That's the life of a developer once you've started abstracting and thinking with logical conditions for long enough. I tend to ask my wife for clarification more times than she'd like, simply because the ambiguity of natural language is something programming has taught me to avoid.

But back to the point—you want to avoid breaking your original code when making the major changes involved in refactoring. That's not because the extracted code would somehow break the existing logic, but because by doing so you'll leave a "logical hole" that needs to be filled. How you fill it will determine the quality of your refactoring.

Imagine having ten lines of code dedicated to greeting the user after they've signed in on your website. Now you need to take those ten lines and turn them into a function, because they can be reused somewhere else. Those ten lines have been removed, and the original logic will no longer greet the user until you fill that empty

---

[1] If you've never read or watched *The Lord of the Rings*, stop right here and go do it. This book will be waiting when you're done.

space with something. That's the logical hole left by refactoring, and when it's filled, you need to ensure the logic remains the same.

What kind of safety net can you use to avoid having your entire team curse you and your descendants for the next three generations? You have a couple of options.

4.2.1 *Version control is your friend!*

Whether you're using Git or SVN or the next fancy version control system that comes along, you need to take advantage of its branching feature. Any software project worth its time will usually have at least one main branch containing the production code. This is the code that ends up being deployed or delivered to users, and it's the branch you don't want to mess with.

You're going to be making some major changes, and they could be so big that they might take you a while to make. Meanwhile, others will be working in parallel, changing other bits of code here and there. Figure 4.1 shows what that looks like from a generic version control perspective.

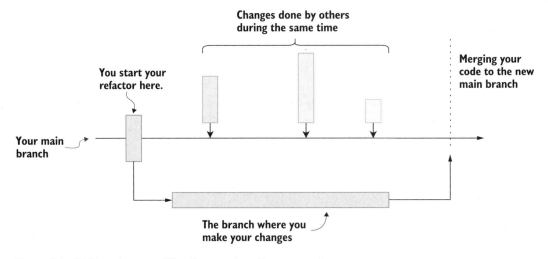

Figure 4.1   Making changes while others work on the same code

The main point of figure 4.1 is that the code you'll be affecting once you're done with your refactoring will not be exactly the same code that you started with. The main branch can't stay frozen for too long—that would mean the entire team is unable to release their work because they're waiting on you to finish. One major benefit of using a version control system is that it provides you with tools to review and understand how merging your changes with the main branch will affect the code as a whole. It's a bit of a pickle, I know, but that's how software development teams work. Everyone keeps moving forward, and your job is to make sure you understand how to mitigate the effect that will have on your work.

One common strategy is to update your code from the main branch every time new code is merged into it, as illustrated in figure 4.2. With this technique, you make sure that you're working on the latest version of the codebase, and most importantly, you make sure that by the time you're finished with your refactoring, your new branch looks a lot more like the main branch of your project. With the scheme in figure 4.1, by the time you were done refactoring, there were at least three major changes in the main branch that you hadn't taken into consideration. With the approach in figure 4.2, you included all those changes, and if they affected your work, you've already dealt with them.

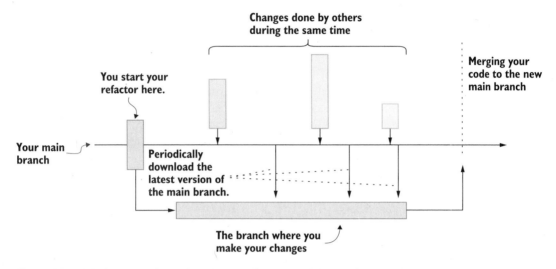

Figure 4.2   Updating your refactor branch every time the main branch is updated

The major drawback of this approach is that you're forced to stop working on your refactoring to accommodate incoming changes every time the main branch is updated. And you'll have to do that often, or the main branch will have diverged so much that you can no longer merge it back into your own without resolving too many conflicts. This will increase your development time and cause you to worry about things other than your refactoring.

Sadly, with a refactoring that takes long enough for your source branch (in this case, the main branch) to be updated multiple times, you will not escape merge conflicts. There's no way around it. Merge conflicts appear when you and others work on the same piece of code and the merging system is unable to understand whose changes take precedence over others'. You're left to decide on your own.

In these situations, it's best to review the changes carefully and, ideally, with the other involved developers, and determine what the best course of action is:

- Do you disregard their changes and accept yours?
- Do you disregard your changes and accept theirs?
- Do you manually mix both changes?

Merge conflicts are a common scenario with big enough teams, so don't stress yourself too much about it. You'll have to deal with conflicts every once in a while. The good news is that there are ways to solve them. Just make sure you communicate with the others involved—there is nothing worse than having your code changes overridden by someone else without them telling you about it.

4.2.2   *Unit tests are all the rage*

We talked about unit tests in chapter 3, and this is a perfect use case for them. In an ideal scenario, a major code refactoring will not affect the business logic of your system (unless that is also part of your aim). This means that from the unit testing perspective, you're not really doing anything. If your tests are structured correctly and decoupled from the implementation of your logic, they should be able to tell you if you've broken anything in the code you've changed.

After all, remember that the purpose of unit tests is to ensure the stability of your system during future code changes. This scenario fits that description perfectly: you're making changes to generalize a section of the logic. Your aim is for your product to remain working while you make your code accessible to others. This means that your current set of tests should need no changes.

This is, of course, an ideal scenario. In reality, some tests might be coupled to the implementation of the logic they're trying to test (such as when spies are used to understand what methods are being called). That's not ideal, but you can still use that to your advantage, because failing tests will signal obvious sections where you've made breaking changes, and you'll need to be extra careful with them.

You'll have to update those breaking tests, of course, but make sure you're extra careful when doing so. Just because a test breaks after a major change doesn't mean the test is no longer valid or that the new logic is completely error free. You have to consider the test update independently of the refactoring you've done and go back to thinking about edge cases, potential unexpected scenarios, or combinations that might not be ideal for the new code you're testing. The worst thing you could do to a test is make it pass based on the behavior of your new code. That would render it useless, because instead of checking for stability, it would now be assuming stability based on a piece of unchecked code. See where the problem resides? A test update required by a code change should be tackled just like you would have tackled it the first time around: independent of the actual results you're getting and focusing on the results you want.

Note that here I'm talking about updating tests that fail after you've made changes to the code. This is not to be confused with the previous section, about using Git branching to merge other people's changes. If their changes broke a set of tests, it should be their responsibility to fix those tests before finishing the push. Expecting you to fix a set of broken tests around code you didn't touch, and that you've potentially never seen before, is not right and should not be how a team behaves. Right now, only worry about tests failing within the context of the changes you're making, not outside of it.

4.2.3 *Baselining your code*

Baselining your code sounds a lot more complex and fancy than it really is. When you're about to perform a major refactoring, it's important to make sure you can undo your changes to a previous stable version. This means taking a picture of your code as it was right before you started working on it.

This step is implied if you're using version control and some kind of branching model, since you can simply ditch your current branch and start over without affecting anything. However, if branching is not an option for some reason, you can create your own branch. Find the most stable version of the code that is currently in production, and make a copy of it right before you start working on it. If you screw up something, or you're unable to get your refactoring to work properly, you can still recover that backup and undo all your problems.

Of course, if you're working on a long refactoring, like in figure 4.1, restoring your baseline will also undo any changes that were added to the original main branch, so consider that as well. A potential fix for this problem would be to keep your baseline copy updated with any changes that have been deployed since you started refactoring. After all, this baseline is just a backup in case your changes break the project.

4.2.4 *I love it when a plan comes together*

Having a plan for your refactoring is not only a great idea, but a must, if you ask me. It's one thing to understand what the end picture should look like (in this scenario, your code should be working with a new external library created by you), and it's a very different thing to know how you're going to get there.

Both have to happen for a successful refactoring:

- You need to understand where you're going and how your changes will impact the overall codebase.
- You have to plan how to get there, especially if the refactoring is big enough (which, in our scenario, it is).

This is just an elaborate way of saying that you can't just decide to refactor your code and then immediately start making changes like there is no tomorrow. A proper refactoring needs to be planned. Consider how many sections of your code will need to be changed, make a list, and review the code in those sections to look for potential problems. Given the right conditions, you might also want to schedule regular code reviews with other developers to catch potential problems before they become major ones. This is especially true if your refactoring affects *their* code—who better to help you understand if you broke something than the original author? Nobody.

The key takeaway here is to remember that you need to follow a plan of action to make sure you've tackled every section, tested every change, and reviewed every line of code before you deem it done.

4.3   *What to focus on when refactoring*

Refactoring for the sake of refactoring makes no sense and will likely yield poor results. Instead, when refactoring, make sure you understand exactly why you're doing it and focus on that. A clear goal is key to successful refactoring. That goal can be anything from fixing a bug to improving the performance of your code. The point is to have an objective, and that objective will guide your refactoring plan.

Let's continue with our refactoring scenario from before: you have to move a section of your code and generalize it into a library that others can use. How will you tackle this task? Is it enough to just copy and paste the code into a new project, and then add the required code to turn it into a library? That might work, but it's also a very short-sighted approach. After all, you originally wrote that code with a very different goal in mind. Given this new context, is it still the best approach possible?

For instance, you wrote the original code thinking about a single use case. Maybe you hardcoded some values, or perhaps you didn't add proper code comments along the way, because you were the only one reading that code. Now you're creating a library, which by definition will be used by many others. Is your code still up to the standards expected by your team?

Your main focus should still be the fact that your code needs to become a generic library that will support your own use case and that of others. But you can also take this opportunity to worry about other details that, especially in this context, will improve the quality of your code: removing code smells.

The concept of "smell" in our context may seem strange at first, but it kind of makes sense. *Code smells* are little problems that don't really stand out by themselves but that give you a funny feeling, like there is something wrong with your code but you can't pinpoint exactly what it is. It's like coming home after a week-long vacation, opening your fridge, and discovering it smells like someone died inside it. Clearly something didn't stand the test of time, but what? You'll have to start a close inspection of whatever is inside your fridge to find what's giving off that terrible smell.

Code smells are exactly like that. Something in your code is giving off a funny smell, but until you take out your magnifying glass and start a close inspection, you won't know exactly what's wrong.

Let's take a look at some common code smells and how you can avoid them.

4.3.1   *Magic values*

Neither of these things are true:

- Other developers can read your mind.
- You have a great memory and can remember why you've written every single line of code in your life.

With that in mind, imagine having to figure out why you used a particular number in the middle of your code, or why you're comparing a variable against the word "action." Those are what I call "magic values"—any piece of data that is directly inserted into the code without any context other than its surrounding code. The following listing shows an example of this.

Listing 4.1 A piece of code with a magic number in it

```
let total_price = 2.04 * price
```
← A number that, by itself, says nothing unless you remember where you got it from

---

Listing 4.1 could mean anything without additional context, and even with the context, the number 2.04 might mean many things. Maybe if you spend five minutes rummaging through your brain, you'll remember what that magic number means, but that's not ideal, is it?

Instead, if you were to store that number in a constant that's properly named (something like MADRID_TAXES), you could use that constant as part of your calculation, and understanding the code would become a lot easier. Take a look at the following listing—would you still need five minutes to understand it?

Listing 4.2 A piece of code with a constant in it

An aptly named constant with the correct value assigned
```
const MADRID_TAXES = 2.04
let total_price = MADRID_TAXES  * price
```
The calculation using the constant instead of the magic number ←

We now can clearly understand the purpose of the calculation. Even if the actual definition of the constant was somewhere else, we're using a value (whatever it might be) in a constant called MADRID_TAXES, so we know all we need to understand the code.

This is why magic values—strings and numbers used for calculations directly in the code—are not recommended. They serve a purpose, but understanding where they're coming from can require a lot of work. Also, if you directly write these values in your code, and later they need to be changed for whatever reason (perhaps the taxes in Madrid dropped 0.4%), you'll have to go looking for where you used them and change each yourself. On the other hand, if you defined them once and then reused the constant, all you would have to do is update a single line of code. See the benefit?

That's not to say you can't *ever* use numbers or strings directly in your code. There are some situations, such as inside a for loop, or accessing the first item on an array, where numbers are appropriate. Those are completely valid scenarios, as in the following listing, where we're using 0 to indicate the first index of our array, or rather, the first index we want to traverse of our array.

Listing 4.3 A valid use case for hardcoded numbers

```
for(let i = 0; i < array.length; i++) {
    console.log(array[i]);
}
```
← A valid use of numbers

This is a normally accepted use of numbers in code, since we all know arrays start at the 0 position (with some very limited exceptions).

4.3.2   *Everyone's doing everything*

In programming, the single responsibility principle ensures that whatever entity you're creating (whether it's a class or a module) concentrates all code required to perform its task within itself. Imagine you're developing an e-commerce site, and you're working on the checkout process. There you could have functionality such as

- Making a payment with PayPal
- Making a payment with a credit card
- Setting a preferred delivery date
- Calculating the actual delivery date of all products

And so on. From a code-organization point of view, you could spread all this functionality across different files, inside different modules or classes, or you could have a single CheckOut class that contains the code required to do all these things.

The single responsibility principle tells us that the correct option is to keep it in a single class, because that way you'll be able to easily find, maintain, and—wait for it—*refactor* any functionality associated with the checkout process. That is what you'll normally want to do when designing and architecting your code.

The other option is to spread that same code throughout a set of entities. This makes it more difficult to maintain the code and make changes to it. It's one thing to modify a single file and a very different thing to have to change four different files.

This is a very common problem with object-oriented code—you'll often have to think about grouping behavior and state together, and for inexperienced developers, that might not be as straightforward as it sounds. But this issue can also come up when you're writing modules that export functions. If they don't make sense grouped together, they shouldn't be in the same module or class.

Consider this when grouping code. Just because you can write it all inside the same file, that doesn't mean you should. If you have four functions, and the best solution is to split them into two and two, then do it. Your future self will appreciate it.

4.3.3   *You're too primitive!*

Overusing primitive values, basic variables, and constants (such as variables of integer or string type, or single characters) to store relevant information is considered a code smell. This is because the related logic needs to be written around these variables. Put another way, you can't abstract logic with primitive values—your code ends up being too low-level, requiring mental parsing to understand it. I'm talking about storing a phone number inside a string variable, and then suddenly needing a date variable to store the user's birthdate—then, a few days later, trying to capture the user's address by using another string variable.

Imagine you have a function that uses all those values to perform internal calculations (such as calculating the age of the user). In the following listing, you can see the underlying logic for those calculations in the function. This is not ideal, especially if the function in question is meant to do something completely different, like save the user to the database.

Listing 4.4　Using primitive values for multiple data points

```
function saveUser(name: string, address: string, birthdate: Date,
    phone_number: string) {
    //...
    let diff_ms = Date.now() - birthdate.getTime();
    let age_dt = new Date(diff_ms);
    let age: number = Math.abs(age_dt.getUTCFullYear() - 1970);

    ///....
}
```

Because we used primitive value types in listing 4.4, the logic required to calculate the user's age also has to be inside the saveUser function. This shows one of the drawbacks of this code smell: your logic is spread across multiple sections. (We added code to calculate the age inside the function that saves the user to the database, but what if you need this code somewhere else?). Sound familiar?

When this is the case (and you have the chance), grouping related logic into a single class simplifies every aspect of this code. Imagine coding a User class that would contain all the relevant information about users, including, of course, the logic required to calculate their age. The following listing shows an example of how you'd implement this class.

Listing 4.5　Every piece of information and related logic inside the class

```
class User {                             The user information is stored
    private name: string;       ←──      privately inside the class.
    private address: string;
    private birthdate: Date;
    private  phone_number: string;
                                          The user-related logic
                                          is inside the class.
    public getAge(): number {   ←──
        let diff_ms = Date.now() - this.birthdate.getTime();

        let age_dt = new Date(diff_ms);
        return Math.abs(age_dt.getUTCFullYear() - 1970);
    }

}                                         The saveUser function is now
                                          oblivious to the underlying logic
function saveUser(usr: User) {   ←──      of the age-calculation method.
    //...
    let age: number = usr.getAge();
    //...
}
```

Listing 4.5 shows how, through the encapsulation of the user data and logic, the client code (the code that uses your data) can be completely unaware of what the implementation looks like. You can keep adding user-related logic to the class, and maintaining it can be as simple as modifying a single class.

4.3.4 *Obsessive use of switch or if statements*

There is nothing wrong with a `switch` statement, and using a few `if`s in your code is not going to kill anybody. However, there is "using," and then there is "abusing." Both statements are great flow control tools that you can use to control how your logic works. But they're meant to be used for simple scenarios, such as a `switch` with a few cases, or an `if` here and there with the occasional `else` clause.

Code like the following makes it very hard to understand, read, and maintain your logic.

Listing 4.6   Abusing the `if`

```
let menuOption = getUserInput();

if (menuOption == 2) {
    //...
} else if (menuOption == 3) {
    //...
} else if (menuOption == 4) {
    //...
} else {
    //if we don't know what to do, we do this
}
```

This code works, and maybe with four cases it can still be readable, but the more logic you write between those curly brackets, the harder it'll get to read and understand it.

We've covered this before: code needs to be readable first, and it needs to work second, so consider using a different approach. Use something that is more declarative than imperative; something that shows what needs to happen instead of describing how it needs to function. The following example is a lot cleaner because it directly maps the logic associated with each menu option to a function. We then select the right piece of logic by referencing the correct array index (which is the menu option selected by the user).

Listing 4.7   Getting rid of the `if`s

```
logicMapping = {
    2: function1,
    3: function2,
    4: function3
}

if(menuOption in logicMapping.keys()) {
```

```
        logicMapping[menuOption]()
} else {
    //... default behavior
}
```

We went from having three `if`s and an `else` clause to only one of each. We can do one better still by implementing the factory design pattern, where we move the decision logic inside a function and hide it from the outside world. The following listing shows what I mean by that.

Listing 4.8   Implementing the factory design pattern

```
//...
function getCorrectMenuLogic(value) {
    let logicMapping = {
            2: function1,
            3: function2,
            4: function3
    }
    try {                           A try/catch statement to
            return logicMapping[value]    capture the only problem
    } catch {                       we might find here
            return defaultFunction
    }
}

//The outside world
let action = getCorrectMenuLogic(menuOption)    The client code doesn't know
action()                                        anything about the strategy
                                                used to pick the right logic.
```

In the `try/catch`, we try to capture the only potential problem we might find in this function: the situation where `value` doesn't have a valid index value for our mapping structure (it's not a valid menu option).

From the user's perspective, the last two code lines (where we get the right menu option and execute it) are a lot easier to understand (they're declarative) than reading a huge list of `if`s. Also, we could change the strategy for selecting the right piece of logic, and the outward-facing code at the end wouldn't have to be affected.

4.3.5   *Duplicated duplicated code*

Duplicated code doesn't just mean the same exact lines of code copied and pasted into another place. Duplicated code also means very similar logic written slightly differently in multiple places. Both are terrible ways of reusing code.

For example, imagine defining a logging function while a colleague working on the same project defines their own version. You'd end up with two similar, yet different, logging functions. Is this code duplication?

Listing 4.9 Duplicated code that doesn't look the same

```
//logging function 1
function logMe(text) {          ◄—— The logging function you defined
    console.log("[LOG]", text)
}


//logging function 2
const fs = require("fs")

function logger(text, level) {     ◄—— The logging function your colleague defined

    if(level == "debug") {
            console.log("[DEBUG]", text)
    }

    if(level == "info") {
        fs.writeFileSync("./logfile.log", text)
        console.log("[INFO]", text)
    }

    if(level == "error") {
        fs.writeFileSync("./error-logs.log", text)
        console.log("[ERR]", text)
    }
}
```

The functions in listing 4.7 are completely different. They even have different function signatures. However, they're meant to do the same thing. This is duplicated code. If you don't tackle this type of duplication, you're making it harder for someone else (or even yourself) to maintain and modify the code in the future.

And don't get me wrong, this can happen even without you realizing it by having multiple developers working on the same codebase. It's just a sign of a lack of coordination, and it happens. The good thing is that, through code refactoring, you can solve that problem.

I like to say, "If you're doing it more than once, then you need to generalize it." Hence, if you have two functions doing something very similar (as in listing 4.7), you need to generalize it, probably by making logger the only function in charge of the logging logic, and replacing all calls to logMe with calls to logger.

The refactoring itself can take the form of extracting code into a function, or collapsing a few methods into one. Whichever approach you take, as long as you keep the logic in one place, it'll be easier for everyone.

Code smells can take many forms and be caused by many reasons. The important thing to understand is that they can be solved, and the sooner you start picking up on them, the sooner the quality of the code you write will improve.

4.4 How to perform code refactoring

Refactoring code is not just about changing the code, it's also about changing designs and architectures. That being said, once you've analyzed and planned everything about the refactoring, it's indeed time to start changing code around.

But going about it manually might not be the best alternative. Not if you have to do major refactoring that can affect multiple sections. Imagine refactoring something simple, such as renaming a class. You may be instantiating that class in 22 files, so you'll have to go file by file and manually change that single line of code. What if you miss one? What if you forget to click Save on a couple more? Manual changes are dangerous and very likely to introduce unwanted errors.

There are tools and best practices for refactoring code, so let's take a look at them before you start moving code around.

4.4.1 Common refactoring techniques

The following techniques will show you some common ways of fixing the problems I've been highlighting in this chapter. You'll likely end up using them so much that they'll become second nature. If you come back to this book in a year or two, you'll be wondering how you didn't know this already.

GENERALIZING PROPERTIES AND METHODS

Cases of duplicated code or logic require generalization, but this is not the only case for generalizing. Consider an object-oriented scenario where you start duplicating properties because you need them in multiple classes. For example, you have a `Student` class with a `birthdate` property, and then you create a `Teacher` class, which also requires a `birthdate` property. Is it better to have two properties that represent the same thing? Or perhaps you should use inheritance and create a generic `Person` class with the `birthdate` property (and maybe others) that the two classes can inherit? Spoiler alert: the correct answer is the second option.

Granted, doing this for a single property might sound like overengineering, but you'll hardly have such a limited coupling when there are common properties between classes. Consider what you're doing, what those classes' responsibilities are, and you'll see that you're repeating more than you thought.

Consider using inheritance if you're in an object-oriented environment; in other environments, consider creating a module with a set of common functions that you can import in multiple places.

CONSOLIDATING BOOLEAN EXPRESSIONS

If you suddenly see multiple Boolean statements that lead to the same result (maybe they all return the same value or call the same function), you might want to consolidate them all into a single statement. The following listing shows multiple potential logic paths that land at the same place (returning `0`).

Listing 4.10   Multiple Boolean expressions that do the same thing

```
function aFunction(aParam, secondParam) {

    if(aParam == null) {
        return 0;
    }

    if(aParam == 0) {
        return 0;
    }

    if(aParam != 0 && secondParam ==0) {
        return 0;
    }

    // now your logic begins...
}
```

The code in listing 4.8 will work just fine, but it seems a bit redundant. The Boolean conditions do not repeat themselves, but the end result does, and that's what we're trying to fix here. Instead, consider aggregating these three statements into a single statement.

Listing 4.11   Single `if` and `return` statements

```
function aFunction(aParam, secondParam) {
    if(aParam == null || aParam == 0 ||(aParam != 0 && secondParam ==0) ) {
        return 0;
    }
    // now your logic begins..
}
```

The key consideration have here is that these conditions should all be grouped with OR, because that's how you would interpret the individual `if`s. As long as one of them is TRUE, the `return` statement should be executed. Thus you should use ORs, not ANDs, which would cause the condition to never be triggered.

REPLACING CONDITIONAL STATEMENTS WITH POLYMORPHISM

Replacing conditional statements with polymorphism is only possible in object-oriented languages. That being said, it's a very useful and elegant way of solving the code smell I mentioned in section 4.3.4, with the excessive use of `if` and `switch` statements.

The following listing shows a class with a method that calculates the selling price of a product with taxes included. The code is not complex. It just adds taxes to a product price based on the product type.

Listing 4.12   Using a `switch` statement to control the logic

```
enum ProductType {        ◁─┐  We use an enum to determine
    BOOK = 1,               │  the type of the product.
```

```
        FOOD = 2,
        CLOTH = 3
}

class Product {
    private type: ProductType;
    private price: number;

    getSellingPrice(): number {

        switch(this.type) {

            case ProductType.BOOK:
                return this.price * 1.1;
            break;
            case ProductType.CLOTH:
                return this.price * 1.3;
            break;
            case ProductType.FOOD:
                return this.price * 1;
            break;
        }
    }
}
```

> **Based on the type, we use a switch statement to determine the selling price.**

This code is valid, but if we keep adding different types of products, we'll have to keep adding more types to our enum variable. Eventually, we'll have to edit the getSelling-Price method to add more case clauses to our switch. It's doable now, but when you have 10 or 20 product types, you'll start regretting this decision.

Worry not, however, because polymorphism provides a very simple solution. You can separate the logic into individual classes with the same method names. By doing this and making sure they all inherit from the same class (and thus have the same inherent type), the individual classes can be used interchangeably by the client code. Take a look at the following listing.

Listing 4.13 Solving the switch problem with polymorphism

The abstract class defines the "shape" our objects will have, so they can be used anywhere.

```
abstract class AProduct {
    protected price: number;

    abstract getSellingPrice(): number ;
}

class Food extends AProduct{
    public getSellingPrice(): number {
        return this.price * 1;
    }
}
```

> **The price needs to be protected so the child classes can access it.**

> **We now have one class per product type.**

```
class Book extends AProduct{
    public getSellingPrice(): number {
        return this.price * 1.1;
    }
}

class Cloth extends AProduct{
    public getSellingPrice(): number {
        return this.price * 1.4;
    }
}
```

We've now gotten rid of the enum variable, because the type is implied in the class. Thus, the logic associated with determining the selling price is not encapsulated within each class. Thanks to polymorphism, we can then use any product type (any instance of the three classes) as if they were of the same type, because they all have the same shape (or, to put it another way, because they inherit from the same abstract class).

If you wanted to take this one step further, you could also consider moving each class to its own file, so you'd have a very clean code architecture. If tomorrow you wanted to add further product types, you'd just create a new file for each one and implement a new class—no need to change the existing code. That, my friend, is what good code design looks like.

GOING FROM RED TO GREEN

The technique of going from red to green relates to your test cases rather than the way you change your code. I strongly suggest that no matter what type of insight you get from this book, and this chapter in particular, you make use of your test cases. Remember to include them as part of your coding practices, every single time.

Going from red to green means making changes so that your tests fail (show red results), and then reviewing the tests to make sure you do what you need to make them pass (get green results). That can translate to updating the tests because they're no longer valid, or it can mean fixing the bugs you introduced when making manual code changes.

Either way, having red tests after a big change is a good thing, because it forces you to double-check your changes. I tend to be very suspicious if the tests don't fail after I refactor. That seems too good to be true, and normally it is. Green tests after refactoring usually are an indication of bad tests not covering the code you just refactored and suggest that your code is now in a Schrodinger's cat kind of state, where it is failing and not failing at the same time. The only sure way of knowing which is true is to "open the box," review it, and add the missing tests.

RENAMING THINGS

I can't end this list without covering the most basic of refactoring technique available: renaming identifiers. If Einstein had been a software developer, I could imagine him saying, "There are only two really difficult things in life: coming up with a unified theory of everything and renaming variables, and I'm very close to finishing number one." Granted, Einstein wasn't a developer, but I would buy a T-shirt quoting him saying that anytime.

The point is that naming things is hard. Whether it's because we lack the time or because we can't think of anything better, we end up naming variables something like `foo` or `bar`, and functions like `doIt` or `handler`. I covered this in chapter 2: names should be mnemotechnic, meaning they should help you remember why you put them there in the first place. A variable named `foo` tells you nothing about it, but if it's renamed to `oPerson`, the same variable lets you know it's an object of class `Person` (assuming that's the naming convention you're going with).

Coding standards can help here, because they cover things like standard ways of coming up with variable names that include information about them, such as prefixing objects with an "o" or interfaces with an "i". They may make sure you use "total" as part of a name when naming a sum of values, or they may require you to prefix names of methods that return data with "get." There are infinite ways you can tackle this; the key is to have a standard documented. As long as you have one and share it with everyone who's going to interact with your code, you've won half the battle.

4.4.2 Tools to reduce human error

You do not want to refactor code manually—not if you can avoid it. This is especially true if the codebase you're changing is composed of multiple files spread throughout several folders, or if you were not the one who wrote it (which is highly likely). In a scenario like that, the chances that you'll forget to update one reference or import statement are very high.

Let's look at two types of tools that can help you in your refactoring tasks, saving you time and considerably reducing the risk of introducing errors to the mix: your own IDE and linters.

YOUR IDE

Your integrated development environment (IDE) is the first thing you need to rely on. Chances are, you will not be developing in a plain text editor such as Notepad; you'll be using an IDE. Whether it's Eclipse (www.eclipse.org), Visual Studio Code (https://code.visualstudio.com), Vim (www.vim.org), or another option, it will already have some refactoring capabilities out of the box, or you'll be able to add them through the use of plugins.

The more specialized the IDE is, the more capabilities it will have. For instance, Eclipse, one of the most common and feature-rich Java editors, can be considered a resource hog, but it also provides some of the most powerful refactoring capabilities out there, because it can interpret and understand your code so well. You can simply right-click a Java class and ask the IDE to change its name, automatically updating all references to it (including places where you import and instantiate it).

The key to this behavior is that the IDE understands the code at a reference level— it can understand where your entities are coming from, their shape (their methods and properties), and their types (whenever possible). The more the IDE understands, the more automation it can provide when it comes to refactoring.

These are some other common actions that the IDE will usually be able to perform:

- *Extracting code into an external function*—By selecting the section of the code that you wish to generalize, the IDE will allow you to turn it into a generic function that you can place wherever you like. The selected code is replaced, automatically, by the function call.
- *Extracting a value into a constant*—Remember that we need to keep magic values out of our code, so this is a usual refactoring action that we can find in IDEs. By selecting a given value (whether it's a string, a number, or something else), you'll get an option to extract it into a constant or a private property (depending on whether you're dealing with an OOP language or not).
- *Translating between entity types*—I'm not talking about turning a number into a string here, but more complex scenarios like turning a function into a class (that is, a method within a brand new class). This task doesn't require a lot of work, but we can automate it with a single click.
- *Renaming a single variable within the current logical scope*—This refers to renaming a single parameter for a class method and having the IDE change the variable inside the scope of the method. Or you could rename a property of a class and have the IDE change all references inside the class's code.

Depending on the language you're using, you might see more options, but they will essentially be variations of the preceding list. Don't get caught up in this. Just make sure you know which options are available, in case you ever need them. Otherwise, you'll find yourself performing these refactorings manually more than once.

LINTERS

Linters are tools I often suggest to my development teams because they provide so many useful tips and can only end up helping in the long run. Basically, linters are tools that will analyze your code and check it against a predefined list of standards. Whether these standards focus on code style (such as how you should write your `if` statements, and whether you should use camel-case instead of snake-case for your variables) or on performance, you can decide what you want the linter to check. Then it will do two things:

- It will highlight all errors it can find in your code, based on your predefined list.
- It will automatically fix as many of these errors as it can safely do.

Normally, linters will find more errors than they can fix, given that some problems are easier to identify than to fix, especially if the solution involves naming things (I've already covered how hard naming things is, remember?). While they won't fix all your problems for you, linters will help you standardize the way your whole team writes code. In the end, your aim is for the code to look like it was all written by the same person (at least as much as practically possible). That way, everyone will know how to read it, where to look for key clues about the logic, and how to expand on it if required.

Linters are tools you normally don't run by hand. Instead, you will add them to the development workflow of your team. Right before you commit your code, the linter should run and make sure your code meets the standards.

Some linters are topic specific, and some are even run for you on platforms such as GitHub. They can check your code for security issues, such as incorrectly structured code, using unchecked user input, or even spotting outdated dependencies that could cause problems.

These are some common linters:

- JSHint (https://jshint.com) and ESLint (https://eslint.org) for JavaScript
- Checkstyle (https://checkstyle.sourceforge.io/config_design.html) for Java
- Rustfmt (https://rust-lang.github.io/rustfmt) for Rust
- Pylint (www.pylint.org) for Python

You can find linters for your own language by Googling them.

Linters are your friends, and while they might seem like an inconvenience at times, such as when they ask you to fix tens or hundreds of small issues every time you want to commit your changes, they are, in fact, helping you code well with others.

And now, let's quickly talk about some best practices that you might want to follow when tackling the refactoring of a codebase, especially when you were not involved with its original version.

4.4.3 *Refactoring best practices*

You'll quickly come to see that in our industry there are millions of ways of doing the same thing. However, there aren't that many *valid* ways of doing it. That is where best practices come into play. If your intention is for your code to be used, reviewed, or even just worked on by others, you need to adhere to the current set of best practices.

There is not just one set of best practices, however; they'll depend on the language you're using or even just your team's preferences. The key thing is for your team to be using the same set at any given point in time.

With that said, I'll identify some generic ones that, with very little imagination on your side, you can apply to your current context.

- *Refactor first, add new features second.* You don't want to add a new feature while you're refactoring code—that should be considered an axiom within our industry. Why? Because both activities require a lot of effort and code changes, and attempting both at the same time might cause a collision of interest. What do you do first? Should you extract a piece of logic that's now required in two different places, or should you duplicate it and make a mental note to refactor it later? Logic would dictate that before working on a new feature, you would want to have the codebase ready for it, instead of having it filled with code smells and anti-patterns, forcing you to work around them to add the new piece of logic.

- *Take advantage of your tests*. This is as much a best practice for developers as breathing is a best practice for your life. This is a must-do for every single project you work on. As I said in the previous discussion of going from red to green, you should expect your tests to fail after a refactoring; it just means you've changed enough code to make them invalid.

- *The QA team needs to be involved*. Even if you already have an extensive and exhaustive test suite, tests will only cover as much as can be automated. Manual testing, especially by experts such as your QA team, is the second-best way to check for anything that your refactoring might have broken. This is especially useful if you have a great unit test suite, but you lack integration tests. Your QA team will be testing everything as users would, so they will be able to catch other types of problems that you might have missed in your tests. Don't get me wrong, this is not a one-off testing job. They should be involved as part of the development process for any change, including (if not especially) big refactorings. Being a good developer is not about writing code that doesn't need to be tested, but rather about (among other things) knowing how to work with testers and taking advantage of their expertise.

- *It will never be perfect, so don't aim for perfection*. There is no such thing as perfect refactorings; they don't exist. You can't predict how the rest of the codebase will evolve, or how the business's needs will change, or how those changes will affect the underlying logic of your project. Stop trying to create the perfect abstraction or to find the best name for your variable. Just make sure that whatever you do now makes sense for your current context and the foreseeable future. The rest will have to be taken care of once you reach that stage.

- *Use the tools at hand, and avoid manual refactors*. Humans are imperfect no matter how much we like to think otherwise. You might think you have a perfect memory, but you'll forget about a class or a function name if you have to change it 30 times within a single day. Instead, rely on the automation provided by both your IDE and linters. They will have your back when you need to perform basic refactoring. Rely on them, and only attempt manual refactoring when it involves design decisions, coordination with other areas, or even major changes that will affect other sections using that code (such as breaking changes that require a lot of adjustments).

Remember, automate as much as you can, and test, both automatically and manually, as much as you can to make sure that whatever you've changed has not diminished the stability of your logic.

4.5   What if you don't need to refactor your code?

Refactoring your code (or anybody else's) is a great way to learn, to practice different coding techniques and design patterns, and to improve the overall quality of the code you work with. Sometimes, however, refactoring code might not be the answer to your problems. That's right, in a chapter about refactoring code, I'm telling you that sometimes refactoring might not be a good idea.

Let's put it this way: refactoring code requires a lot of effort, and it can potentially affect a lot of the work others have done in the past and code that others might be using right now. You have to be very sure when you start refactoring that it will be cost effective. You need to be sure the effort you'll go through will bring the expected benefits.

Now that the warnings are out of the way, let's consider some "crazy" scenarios where you would not want to refactor code:

- *The code just doesn't need to be refactored.* Clean code is the goal for all of us, but let's be real for a second; it's not always required. When you're wondering if you should start the refactoring you have in mind, ask yourself the following two questions: Is this code in production already? Will it be changed in the future, or is this code something nobody will work on again? If it's in production and isn't likely to be changed, refactoring is neither useful nor cost effective. The trouble you'll go through and the time it'll take are both too much.

- *Your changes will not make it easy to add future features.* A lie we sometimes tell ourselves is, "I'm doing this so that it'll be easier for us to add new features in the next release." That's not true unless you already know which features you'll be working on. What you're doing is guessing about how you'll need to architect your code once the actual business requirements arrive. If you're lucky, your refactoring will actually make sense, but if you're not (which would be 90% of the time), you'll have to either revert the refactoring or implement new refactoring to undo your last changes. Don't refactor based on assumptions; find out what's coming and only then start planning for it.

- *Your refactoring won't fix any problems.* This scenario is a very common one. We tend to think that code that doesn't follow our own standards is likely to be faulty. However, changing code simply for the sake of changing it makes no sense. You have to consider the standards provided by your team and whether the changes you want to implement are covered there. Only then ask yourself this: "Will I be adding actual value?" "Value" can refer to many things, but it does not mean "I'm making it better because I say so." Don't force your own opinion about how others should be coding. Stick to the standards everyone is meant to be following (including you).

- *It's not your code.* This refers to the particular scenario where you're considering contributing to a codebase that you're not part of, such as an open source project or a project from another team inside your company. Either way, those projects are following their own coding standards. Refactoring their code to meet your own standards not only makes no sense, but it can also be considered a very rude move. Imagine me moving into your house and forcing you to become vegetarian just because a vegetarian diet has done wonders for my health, so I think it should have the same effect on you. That's what you would be doing to these other maintainers if you force your own refactoring into their code without asking permission. Instead, consider asking if you could work on such a refactoring and explain why you think it would add value to their project. If you manage to sell them on the idea of the code change, then congrats, but if you're told "no," don't insist and move on.

- *The small refactoring you propose implies a huge impact on the rest of the system.* The easiest way to visualize this is to consider a microservice-based architecture where you have multiple mini projects talking to each other through APIs. These APIs act as contracts between two services, and they also force the implementation of the logic required to interact with them. A small change that ends up requiring an update to the public API means a change in that contract, which in turn means you're forcing a code change on every piece of software relying on that contract. That can mean you're forcing a single project to update their code or hundreds of other projects to update theirs. In this scenario, you have to weigh the added value of your refactoring against the impact it'll have on your and other teams.

Code refactorings are very useful, but they are not always the right way to go. Remember to think about these three things before deciding whether or not to start refactoring:

- How much value is your change adding?
- What's the impact of your change?
- Do you have enough time to refactor the code without affecting your team's timeline?

Consider the answers to those questions and decide whether or not refactoring is the right move.

Summary

- Before you start any refactoring, you need to understand how to version control your code, how to baseline it so that you can come back to it if there is a problem, and to always have unit tests around the piece of code you're changing. That way, you have everything you need to either roll back any breaking changes or avoid breaking changes by checking that everything works after the refactoring is ready.
- Code smells are probably the main thing you'll be looking for in your career, not only while refactoring your code, but while actively coding it. Keep an eye out for things like magic values, spreading responsibility all around your code, and duplicated logic, and you'll improve the quality of your code in no time.
- You don't have to do all your refactoring by hand. An effective refactoring is one that's done without unwanted side effects. How do you achieve that? By relying on the power of automation. The more you can rely on automation for simple refactoring, the less error prone it will be. Stick to manual refactoring when the changes are big enough that they can't be automated.

- Finally, don't overdo it. If you're considering refactoring a piece of code, make sure it makes sense to change it. Scenarios like refactoring other developers' projects, or refactoring code simply for cosmetic reasons (restructuring code to make it look "nicer") are not worth the time and effort they require. Instead, focus on adding value through your refactoring.

Tackling the
personal side of coding

5

This chapter covers

- What it means to "learn how to learn"
- The importance of side projects and why you should consider having at least one
- How making mistakes is good for you
- Why writing is great for developers

The previous chapters have covered what I think are the minimum requirements for starting your journey toward becoming a successful software developer. We've touched on everything you should worry about getting right and what you should focus on versus what you can ignore for the time being.

However, soon you'll start noticing that software development starts taking over your life (if it hasn't already). This happens to most of us. If you're into development, you almost certainly love problem solving, and there is nothing worse than going home and leaving an unresolved problem.

As you're eager to improve and learn more, you'll start spending more and more time reading and watching tutorials, working on side projects, catching up on

#TechTwitter (a popular hashtag on Twitter for discussing tech-related topics) or many of the other activities that can make you feel connected to your journey outside of work. And while these activities aren't bad per se, they can definitely hurt you in the long run. Ironic, isn't it? How can the thing you do to improve work against you? This chapter is dedicated to answering that question and to showing you ways of improving your skills in all important aspects.

And I don't want to spoil the fun or anything, but most of that revolves around a very loaded term: work/life balance. I know, it's a buzzword, but not everyone knows exactly what it means. Because it's such a loaded term, I wanted to cover it in this chapter, among other things.

5.1 How are you learning?

You'll never stop learning. I've covered this point before, but sometimes people think I'm exaggerating, so it's good to reiterate it. Learning will be a constant for as long as you consider career improvement a must, so it's crucial that you have a sound learning strategy. Not only that, but you should also normalize the fact that you'll need it every day.

However, let's focus on "now" for the time being. You're probably either just getting started or working in one of your first job opportunities, and you'll likely find yourself Googling the most basic concepts. Every few days, you'll have to remind yourself how to use the `forEach` method of arrays, how the scope works for that private variable with the closures in JavaScript, or even why you would want to have private properties in your classes.

After a few months of this, that horrible voice in the back of your head starts sounding louder and louder, making you feel like you're doing something wrong: "You better hide this from your teammates, or they'll discover you're a fraud."

This is a very common scenario—so much so that if I were a betting man, I would bet that 99% of all developers go through this at the start of their career (and some still feel this way years later). It's called *impostor syndrome*, and we all have to deal with it at some point.

How you're learning can help you mitigate that voice to some degree, so let's analyze two very different learning practices: self-learning and formal education.

5.1.1 You're not supposed to know everything

The school system taught us that to solve a problem or to be deemed "worthy" of a good grade, we had to be able to answer questions without help from anyone. While this situation might vary from country to country or from school to school, most "standard" education revolves around memorizing facts that you can later use to solve problems or answer questions.

The real world is different, however. The real world is focused on results, and not so much on how you get there, so the first thing you need to accept is that you can ask for help. That can take many forms:

- Asking a teammate to help you solve a problem or to explain how a piece of code works
- Googling for examples of how to solve a particular problem
- Buying an online course for a set of technologies that you've never used before

And there are many other ways for you to learn by yourself. That's the key: by getting this help, you're learning. Nobody expects you to know everything you need to know on your first day of work. This is true at all levels, but especially if you're just getting started.

The learning process, which can take any shape or form and is unique for every developer, has one main objective: to give you autonomy. When you're starting out as a developer, you'll be dependent on others. Your manager will have to give you detailed instructions on what you need to do, and will be checking up on you often. You'll want to ask your more experienced teammates about the tasks you've been assigned and how they would solve them (or have solved them) to get ideas and examples you can use on your own. This is both normal and expected.

But everyone will expect that you will become more and more autonomous over time. Once you've solved a type of problem a few times, everyone will expect that you've learned how to do it without asking so many questions or needing so many detailed instructions. Now, I know what you're thinking: "This section is called 'You're not supposed to know everything,' but I'm being told I need to learn and know things quickly." However, that's not what I said. Yes, you need to become more autonomous, but remember what I said before: the real world focuses on the results, not on the journey.

Becoming autonomous can mean anything—only you know what that means for you. I personally recommend focusing on learning how to learn, instead of focusing on memorizing the details your teammates give you.

The expectation will be that every time you're asked to solve a problem, you first exhaust all self-learning options (within a reasonable amount of time) and only then resort to your colleagues. Why? Because if you can solve problems on your own, you're showing you can tackle new tasks without using others' time to do so.

Learning to learn can involve learning the best sources of information for the technology you're using. It can also mean learning to distill problems to basic (or focused) questions so you can better research the topic at hand.

For instance, suppose you're asked to build a microservice with Python to handle purchase orders on an e-commerce site your team is building. This is your first time doing so, which means you have two options:

- You ask for guidance from a teammate.
- You bury your head in Google and try to figure out how to build a microservice using Python.

The second option may sound better to that little voice in the back of your head, but the query is too generic: "how to build a microservice using Python" can return way too many unrelated results. You'll discover that there are multiple frameworks you could potentially be using and many standards to follow, so you'll have to start making assumptions, making decisions based on them, and, probably, making mistakes.

Instead, if this is your first time, the first option would be the right choice. Ask someone else who's done this in the past, but ask with the intention of learning. Ask for things such as these:

- A code walkthrough of an existing service so you can see the internal structure and frameworks used
- A written guideline, if there are any, detailing the standards to follow when building a microservice within this project
- A list of standards and technologies used to build other microservices

That approach will give you the tools you need to use, and you can then learn how to operate them on your own.

In contrast, you might ask for things such as these:

- A copy of the code so you can modify it to meet your needs
- Help coding the basic structure so you can fill in the rest
- An example of code that shows you how to solve one particular task inside your microservice

These are all solutions, but while they might yield faster results, they could also harm you more than they help you. Don't get me wrong; a lot of people can learn from examples, as long as they use them with the right intentions. The key is to focus on growing your autonomy. With that in mind, which of the following do you think will give you more autonomy in the long run?

- Learning from these examples and then working on a solution on your own?
- Copying and pasting these solutions, and then making quick changes to get them to work without really understanding why they work.

The second option definitely will get you your results sooner, but which approach would you go for? Results are important, but ultimately you'll have to get there on your own as much as possible.

The right answer, in case you were wondering, is the first one: learning from examples will provide the autonomy I'm talking about. This process will take years rather than weeks. As long as you tackle problems this way, learning will become second nature, and the autonomy you're looking for will come on its own. Eventually you'll learn a key secret that all senior developers know: there is no problem you can't solve, because you have the internet on your side. It's a compendium of all human knowledge, so all you need to know is how to find the right answer. You need to learn how to learn, and that's a skill on its own.

5.1.2   *The internet is great, but so is a formal education*

In chapter 1, I mentioned that one of the most common "requirement" misconceptions for starting out as a developer is having a formal education. You don't need to wait three or four (or more) years to get your first job—not when you can get the basics directly from a bootcamp or the internet. However, once you've started on your journey, there is definitely something to be said for going through formal education.

Everyone learns differently. Some people learn by doing, and others need to watch how things are done to understand them. Some will be more comfortable learning at their own pace and following their own interests, while others might require the constant pressure and follow-up of a teacher.

The internet is great, and it contains everything you need to know about anything, but you also have to be your own teacher. If you're the type of person who learns better when there is someone in front of you—someone you can ask a question or ask for help when you need to—a formal education is something you should consider.

I'm not making this up. I learned programming on my own with a very limited internet connection when I was 14 years old. By the time I was 20 and got my first developer job, I started realizing that my self-learning program had been full of holes. I knew how to write code, and I was doing my job well enough, but others around me were talking about design patterns, MVC, and common best practices, and I was looking at them trying to keep my jaw from dropping.

It took me five years, but I eventually decided to get a formal education. I felt I needed to learn about things I had never deemed worth it, and I was right. After five years of work experience, I joined a three-year program, and by the time I was 28 years old, I was a programming analyst. I wasn't an engineer, but I had learned the core concepts that I had skipped over while learning on my own.

And you know what? The core concepts were important, but not for the reason you'd think. Yes, three years later I knew things I didn't before, and that was useful. But by learning those concepts, I had managed to do something a lot more powerful: I had silenced the voice in my head telling me I wasn't good enough. I was now able to talk about the same concepts my colleagues were discussing, and while the quality of my code had improved, I had also gained the confidence I needed to tackle bigger and more complex problems. I had become more autonomous.

I also picked up other skills I had never thought useful for our profession, such as technical writing. I had to write so many papers during those three years that I realized I liked writing. That eventually led me to writing technical articles, and it helped me improve my communication skills.

So, yes, a formal education might not look like it's worth your time, especially an expensive education, but it might be just what you need to take your career to the next level. The specifics in your case might be different; maybe you don't need to know about the core concepts, but you lack formality in your study process. Maybe you're trying to learn everything, but you don't know if you're going in the right direction. A formal education can help solve all those problems and give you the tools you'll need in the future to keep learning on your own. Or maybe you'll discover that you need to keep going back and trying higher forms of education (such as getting a masters or a PhD). Don't discard formal education; not until you've tried it, anyway.

5.2 Side projects

Are you even a developer if you don't have a GitHub account filled with unfinished side projects? Yes, you are, no matter what others might say. As long as you're able to write code, you're a developer, and don't let anyone tell you otherwise.

Side projects are not mandatory, and because they're done outside of working hours, they can eat up hours of personal time. The more time you spend on side projects, the less time you'll have to relax, spend time with friends and family, and do all those other things humans are known for.

So why are we even discussing side projects? Well, they do serve a purpose. Consider the scenario from the previous section, where you find yourself Googling the most basic concepts. To get past this stage, one of the things you decide to do is to work on side projects, hoping that you'll be able to practice those things you're constantly Googling.

What kind of project can you build? How can you decide what to work on and for how long? Let's talk about this.

5.2.1 The case for side projects

Let's step away from the coding world for a second and take a look at Olympic athletes (stay with me, it'll make sense in a minute). Olympic athletes are the best in the world. They take their sports to the limit by breaking them apart, analyzing every bit of them, and then working on their skills every single day. Their sport is their life; it's not a hobby they picked up last year, and it's definitely not something they do as an afterthought. They breathe it while they're awake, and they dream about it when they're asleep.

If you're hoping to be the best developer you can be, you should consider applying a similar training program to your programming skills. I'm not talking about forgetting life and focusing only on coding, but rather about doing learning in a smart way. Optimize the time you have, and train smart—become an Olympic coder, if you will.

This is where side projects come into play (it took a while, but we got there). Side projects are a fantastic way of improving your skills (especially if you haven't had any work experience thus far):

- They allow you to work on things you haven't worked on before, thus expanding your figurative horizon.
- They give you a repertoire of projects to show to potential employers. This comes in very handy when you have little or no work experience to put on your resume. Someone looking to hire you for a developer job will want to know what kind of code you can write, and while they can get you to do some coding tests (something we'll cover in chapter 6), you can provide them with samples as part of your application.

I've suggested side projects to many new developers, and, more often than not, the answer I get is along the lines of "I can't think of anything interesting and original to work on; everything's been done already." That's where you get it all wrong. Side projects aren't meant to be original, innovative, or groundbreaking. You're not looking to disrupt the software development industry; you're looking to learn a new skill, so focus on that.

That means you don't need to be original, so copy someone else's project for instance, or their idea. In fact, I would argue that trying to reproduce someone else's project is a great way to start, because you're not under pressure to come up with every feature that needs to be included or to decide what each one should do. That work has already been done by the owner of the project; all you have to do is reverse-engineer their implementation. After all, you're doing this to improve your tech skills, not your product design skills. That's the beauty of it—it allows you to focus on the code without having to worry about anything else.

If that doesn't sound appealing, maybe try some other options:

- Are you looking to get into game development? Pick up a game that can be modded, such as Minecraft, and start whaling at it. It's a great way to learn Java while you're also learning how to code. Other games that are great alternatives if you're not into open world LEGOs are Civ5, XCOM 2, The Sims 4, and Skyrim, to name just a few. Modding is the perfect way of understanding how game development works, without having to do the whole game-design process.

- If you're more into web development, building a blogging site is an alternative. There is a lot more than meets the eye when it comes to building a blog. You have to consider the ability to create content while being authenticated as a valid user; you have to understand how to deal with content formatting; you have to learn about search engine optimization (SEO) and how that affects your HTML code; and lots more. Consider building a full blogging platform if this is something you're interested in, because you'll also have to learn multiple technologies that are very relevant in today's market (JavaScript, HTML, CSS, HTTP, and some form of backend language, to name a few).

- Are you into robotics? What about getting a cheap Raspberry Pi and some servo motors? You'll be able to code in Python and control physical elements. It's a fun way to get into this field. You could even get some sensors and build some interactivity into your project.

Whatever you work on, make sure it's something you're passionate about, because you'll be using personal time to do so. During that process, you'll face challenges you've never faced before, and you'll grow your skills by problem solving your way through them.

Make sure your code is published somewhere. If you have access to GitHub, open up a public account and push your progress there. If for any reason you can't do that, find a way to share your progress, such as publishing on Medium.com, creating a free site on Wordpress.org, and so on. There are multiple ways for you to share what you've done and how you've done it without spending a dime. By sharing your progress, you'll be able to show others what you've done, how you work, and what you know. This is a fantastic business card that people can get to know you from.

The other, often overlooked, benefit of having side projects to show is that you're also showing others you're capable of finishing something. This is no small feat, trust me. Anyone can start a side project; it's as simple as creating a folder and a readme file with some basic description of what you'll be doing there. Hardly anyone, however, is disciplined enough to close a project. They forget that closing a project is not just about coding. It also includes the following:

- Closing all pending features (which, yes, requires coding)
- Documenting the intention of the project well enough for others to understand
- Releasing a final version of your library (whether it's a compiled DLL file, a JAR file, or whatever form it may take)

Bonus points accumulate if you also create some articles, videos, or some form of content that others can benefit from. Your learning experience can enlighten others as well as you. Explaining problems you've dealt with and how you managed to solve them is also a good way to cement your learning and even help you deepen the understanding you have about the topic.

5.2.2 *What's wrong with side projects?*

How can you accomplish everything I just mentioned without completely destroying your personal life in the name of improvement? That's the key, isn't it? The first thing that goes down the toilet is your "me" time. That leaves you with less time to relax and more likelihood of burning out.

Burnout is real. You can think of it as the exact opposite of how you feel the moment you decide that your personal time is not worth keeping. Right then, you're so excited about your side project and everything you'll accomplish that nothing else matters. Then, when burnout hits, anything else is more important than coding. You just don't have the energy for it, whether it's your job, your side project, or helping a buddy. It doesn't matter, you're done with it. And if you had a timeline to keep, that timeline is in trouble because there is no way you'll stick to it.

What can you do? Pace yourself. Don't think that you have to go all in or it won't work. As I mentioned before, be smart about it:

- *Keep track of your time*—There are many tools out there that can help you keep track of the time you spend doing something. Use them, set yourself a reasonable time limit per week (make sure you leave time for noncoding activities), and stop when it's time to stop.
- *When you do work, work like there is no tomorrow*—Focus on what you're doing, and don't work while watching TV or Netflix. Close your social media, put your phone on airplane mode, and focus on your current task. That way, you'll make the most of your time.

- *Working every day for small amounts of time is a lot better than doing it all on a single day*—Thirty minutes a day, every day, won't kill your free time, and even if you feel like you're not making any progress, you'll feel a lot better than if you work four or six hours on a Sunday. You'll probably make the same progress project-wise, but in one scenario you're not compromising your mental health, and in the other you're probably neglecting other activities for the sake of finishing your pending work. This can only lead to you not enjoying your weekends and eventually skipping the only day you wanted to work, because by then you're just tired and burned out.

Side projects are great. They can help a lot, especially for new developers, but they're also a double-edged sword. It's very easy to get carried away and compromise your personal time. Keep an eye out for that, and be smart about it. Work on your side projects and improve your skills, but don't pay for it with your free time.

And if all of this sounds like too much or it just doesn't appeal to you, that's fine too. Side projects are not mandatory. You're perfectly fine if you're only coding during your working hours.

5.2.3   *What about working on open source projects?*

Open source is probably one of the best things to ever happen to our industry. The way developers collaborate with each other, making their projects better and more robust, is something that you don't see in any other industry. However, many people consider this to be a waste of time. Why spend time and effort working on someone else's project? That's a fair question to ask, but there are certainly some benefits to doing so.

A word of caution though: there are good places for you to contribute and learn, and there are also bad places, where your contributions and questions won't be well received. Just because a project is marked as open source doesn't mean its creators are eagerly looking for outside help. Be careful where you choose to spend your time trying to help.

That being said, there are easy ways to spot the good projects that are looking for help, and even ones that are open to new junior contributors, so let's focus on those.

WHY CONTRIBUTE TO OPEN SOURCE?

From the perspective of someone who's just getting started and looking to learn as much as possible, contributing to an open source project can bring benefits in several areas. From a technical point of view, you'll face challenges such as these:

- *Reviewing someone else's code*—Learning how to read code is very important. Through this practice, you can learn what easy-to-read code looks like and what spaghetti code looks like. I've been saying it throughout this book: your code needs to work on a computer, but it also needs to be read by humans. This exercise will show you examples of that. You will also pick up on techniques and methodologies you weren't aware of by reading code from others more experienced than you.

- *Getting bug reports that you never thought about*—Whether it's your own project or someone else's, you'll be looking at bug reports as a potential source of contribution ideas. You'll see problems that you've never encountered before, like memory leaks, race conditions, and other things that happen when you take a piece of code to the very limits of its design. If you're just working on your own side project without real use-case scenarios, you might never encounter real-world problems such as these.

- *Getting your code reviewed by others*—Just as important as knowing how to read code is knowing how to take criticism and how to accept a recommendation or an idea about how to improve your code. As much as you can help a project with your contributions, the project itself will benefit *you* by pushing you to grow as a developer, to apply better standards, and to learn new techniques. This is one of the major benefits of contributing to open source projects.

- *Following coding standards*—For your contributions to be accepted, you'll have to follow certain project-wide standards. That's reasonable, considering that whoever is going to review your code needs to know how to read it. In the end, even though the project might have hundreds of contributors, the code should look like the same person wrote the whole thing. This is great preparation for working as part of a team in a company.

- *Git, Git, and more Git*—Currently, Git is the version control standard that most open source projects use. This means that for you to be able to work with them, you'll have to learn about Git. Guess who else uses Git? Almost every other software company in the world. By learning Git, you're not learning a new skill that you'll only use outside of work; rather, you're getting used to working with one of the main tools in any development project.

From an organizational perspective, you'll get the following:

- *Insight into running a complex project*—This won't happen from running your own side projects. However, you'll experience organizational hazards by contributing to large open source projects. Some of them have committees to evaluate who gets to contribute and who doesn't, or what the project's future looks like. Some of these projects are 10 minutes away from suddenly turning into companies on their own, so their internal procedures resemble a lot what you'll find working for someone else.

- *Autonomy*—Open source projects don't really have managers who will spend their time following up on you and checking how you're doing. You either work on your contribution, following all standards and guidelines, or you don't. Nobody really cares if you quit mid-feature; someone else will pick up where you left off, or will start over. It's kind of a swim or sink situation, so you'll have to push yourself and learn by yourself—that's a skill every manager wants their team members to have!

- *Flexibility*—If you like the experience and start contributing to several open source projects, you'll have to be flexible when it comes to the way you work. Not every project will require the same processes or the same coding standards. The more alternatives you see, the more flexible your process will become. This, in turn, makes you a great asset when it comes to finding new profiles for new projects within a company.

You will be helping projects by contributing your work (in whatever form that work might take), but the one getting the most out of this interaction will be you. You get to learn, you get feedback, and you get to experience new ways of working.

It might be scary at first, thinking you're not good enough to contribute to a big library or framework, but anything you can bring to the table (even a simple typo correction in the documentation) will be received with an open mind and the intention of making something great even better. This is the main philosophy behind open source and why I always recommend new developers try to contribute to at least one project if they have the time. It's an experience you have to go through.

How to pick the right open source project

Once you've made up your mind and decided you will contribute to a project, you have to find the right one. The internet is filled with open source projects because pushing code to a public place is easy and free. That said, not all projects are looking for contributors. Some developers will clearly let you know in their main documentation file (usually called readme.md) that they're not looking for external help, or what the process for contributing looks like.

If there are no guidelines, I recommend staying away from trying to contribute, unless, of course, you've identified a bug in their code and already have the fix for it. In such a scenario, I would try to directly contact the author and ask for permission to create a pull request (essentially a merge request of your branch into their main branch). That is the bare minimum etiquette you'll have to follow in such a situation.

If, on the other hand, you do not have a particular project in mind, you might want to look at some of the libraries and frameworks you use in your daily work. Most of them will have a contribution process in place, and some will go so far as to tag issues and bug reports specifically for newcomers. Tags such as "good first issue" are indicative of a project that's perfect for a newcomer like you. The Node.js project, for instance, does this (https://github.com/nodejs/node/issues). If you see something like that, consider reading it. Sometimes these will be very focused changes, or even documentation updates. The point of those issues is to get you started in the process. Once you know how that part works, you can start looking for more interesting and relevant contributions.

Finding such projects is not easy, but luckily for you, there are people who have already been through this and decided to create some online help for developers like you. The main place where you can get the information you need is "First Timers Only" (www.firsttimersonly.com). It contains a list of different places where you can find the perfect first open source project to contribute to.

Wherever you end up pushing your code, always remember the following:

- Be polite. You're getting as much (if not more) out of this interaction as the code owners are.
- Understand that getting a response might take time. They're not sitting there waiting to get contributions. The owners of these projects have lives too.
- Follow every single point in their guidelines. If they're there, it's for a reason. Don't try to skip steps because you think you know better.
- Have fun throughout the process. You're doing this mainly to learn and improve your skills, but it doesn't have to be boring. There are plenty of projects out there that are looking for help. Find one that makes you want to help out.

Whatever you decide to do about this, remember, there should be a balance between how much work you put into these projects and the rest of your life. If you put too much effort into these projects and neglect other areas, it's not going to be worth it in the long run.

5.3 Asking your online friends for help

We as developers can't function without access to the internet; it's just not practical. The internet has all the information we need, and when we can't find it, we can ask others for help. Unfortunately, not everyone out there is willing to help. The anonymity of different social networks sometimes brings out the worst in people and makes them think they're better than others.

Sadly, a common scenario I faced multiple times while learning how to code was finding a community of developers who were sharing information with each other but would not accept newcomers. Instead of helping newcomers, they would laugh and make jokes about the lack of knowledge I had. Back then, they were forums; today we have communities on sites such as Reddit, Hacker News, Twitter, and even Facebook, where many developers still indulge in such terrible gatekeeping against newcomers.

This is one of the reasons why some developers are not inclined to publicly share their work while learning—many others will laugh at their mistakes instead of focusing on the great progress they're making. This is yet another way in which coding can affect our lives, not because it takes too much time, but because we're leaving the door open to that kind of negative energy.

A lot of newcomers joining online communities are told they're not yet a developer. The excuse may be lack of professional experience, or lack of knowledge, but whatever the reason, it's wrong. If you can write a line of code and make it work, you're a developer. Period. Own it. Don't let anyone else online determine your future by digitally stepping on you. They have no right to do so, so ignore them and keep pushing.

5.3.1 Making mistakes

Everyone learns differently, but a very common way we humans learn is by blundering. Making mistakes and suffering the consequences shows us what not to do, so that next time we face a similar situation, we know what to avoid and to try something different.

Mistakes are not a bad thing. In fact, they're a teaching mechanism, and if we learn how to take advantage of them, we'll be constantly improving, even when we break things. The trick to taking advantage of mistakes is not hard. Thomas Edison said, "I have not failed. I've just found 10,000 ways that won't work." Is that the statement of a loser or a genius? He literally flipped the meaning of failure to be success. Every single "no" put him one step closer to the final "yes" he was looking for.

If you want a more contemporary and on-topic example, take a look at Elon Musk with SpaceX. He wanted SpaceX to be the first company to land a booster rocket after a successful mission (previously, boosters would land uncontrollably in the ocean). This meant pushing the current state of technology to its limits and then going further. Every failed test meant a rocket would be destroyed, but there was no other way of testing, so they took advantage of that. Every test was measured from every potential angle, and every sensor in place was giving SpaceX telemetry about a particular system.

According to interviews, the first Falcon booster to land correctly was the very last attempt that SpaceX had money for. Had it failed, they would have had to close their doors. However, after every failed attempt, they corrected their mistakes (thanks to the telemetry they had received) and tried again. Every "no" put them closer to landing that day, because they were smart about it. They were learning from their mistakes in order to avoid them in the future.

That is why we, as developers, need to make lots of mistakes (being smart about it too), because that is one of the best ways for us to learn. The key here is to fully accept that failing to meet our end goal is an option, because we're making small gains along the way. Every time you get a compiler error, or every time your algorithm doesn't work exactly as you had expected, there is always something to gain. You have to avoid listening to your internal voice telling you that you're never going to make it, and you also have to ignore those online gatekeepers who think they have the right to tell you if you're good enough or not.

The term gatekeeper, in this context, refers to people who consider themselves the absolute owners of the definition of the word "developer." They think they know enough to decide who gets the title and who doesn't. That, of course, is nothing more than an illusion, but gatekeeping is sadly a very common practice in our industry. The anonymity provided by social networks allows for people like that to reach those who do not know better (like new developers). The best way to fight them is to ignore them. Do not engage with them, and do not accept what they tell you—just do your thing, and keep learning and finding ways to improve. As long as you do that, you'll solve every single challenge you face.

5.3.2   *Avoiding the naysayers*

Some online communities are better than others. In general, my online experience has been positive. I've met a lot more people who wanted to help than those who didn't. And, eventually, I also learned to ignore or even block the gatekeepers, since there is no point in listening to what they have to say.

If you have the chance, getting yourself into a nurturing community will provide a lot of benefits. Sadly, there is no whitelist of communities you can use. You'll have to test them out and see for yourself. For example, local meetups are all the rage right now, and they're usually very focused, small groups of developers who have similar interests. And while there might be one or two gatekeepers in there, the majority will be interested in helping others, so they're a good option. If you don't know whether there are any such groups in your area, you can go to Meetup (www.meetup.com) and find something nearby. Local conferences are also very good places to network and meet other developers in person, but they're not as common, and some of them can be very expensive to attend.

When it comes to online spaces, I've personally had good luck with Twitter, especially around the #TechTwitter hashtag. Many developers following that tag are eagerly looking to help others, either with online moral support or actual help with code. That community is very aware of the perils of gatekeeping, so it is a very safe place for newcomers to ask questions and get help. If you're not there yet, give Twitter a chance.

In any case, the point of these communities is to help each other to learn and grow. As a general rule of thumb, if the feedback you get is not constructive, ignoring it is probably the safest bet.

The same goes for you: do not become a naysayer three months into your journey. Keep your ego in check and try to give as much feedback as you would like to receive. Try to be as constructive as you want others to be with you. Otherwise, you'll never find a community that suits your expectations. Everyone is looking for the same thing you are, so the only thing to do is to all contribute in the same capacity.

5.4 *Learning to communicate with others*

Throughout this chapter, I've talked about learning, places to learn, the attitude you should have toward learning, and how to make the most out of your learning experiences. The last thing I want to cover, which will also help improve the way you learn, is getting better at communicating with others. Hear me out.

Knowing how to communicate with others is a skill you *need* to learn. Having great communication skills makes for great developers. Someone who can explain the development plan to a nontechnical person so they understand what's at stake, why the timeline looks like that, and why they have to pay twice as much as they thought is a great asset on a development team. And there is no better way of developing these skills than jumping into the communication waters.

There are two main types of communication: direct and indirect. *Direct* communication involves you being in front of your target audience, whether that's a single person or a room filled with hundreds. We're talking about internal technical presentations for other tech teams in your own company, or coaching a colleague who's just getting started, or perhaps presenting a talk at a programming conference. These are all great ways for you to practice communicating complex topics in simple terms. It's not an easy thing to do, but by doing it, you're showing what you know about a particular topic. Whether you're an expert on the subject or you research the heck out of it for the presentation, you'll look like an expert to your audience. And if you don't think so, consider the last time you were on the receiving end of one of these talks. Did you consider them experts? You did, didn't you? Good direct communication skills can help you achieve this.

Of course, if you're introverted (like me), you're probably having a small anxiety attack just reading this. And I get it, I was there too. But trust me, while presenting might not be something you do regularly, you need to be able to step up and explain a complex concept when needed: your team might need it, or your manager might request it. Whatever the reason, you need to be ready.

On the other hand, you might prefer to try and work on your *indirect* communication skills. Don't think that just because you're not in front of people it's less relevant or less difficult to develop. You can work on this skill by writing articles, creating videos, building online courses, or however you like. My personal recommendation would be to try blogging. Why? Because it's the cheapest way of starting—you don't need a lot of software, and you can get started and publish your first article in two hours (or less).

Either way, by taking the plunge, you'll start working on a skill that most developers ignore. This will, in turn, set you apart from the rest. And the best part of it? The more you write and the better you get at it, the better you'll also get at speaking. Explaining complex concepts orally will be easier, thanks to your writing experience. So while you're focusing on your indirect communication skills, you'll indirectly improve your direct communication skills as well. As long as you focus on developing your ability to explain technical concepts to others, you'll be improving all aspects of your communication, both direct and indirect.

Don't underestimate this communication practice. This is as important as working on your coding skills. I think that every developer interested in improving their career must work on this. I'm not saying, "Go and become an online influencer." All I'm saying is, "Get a blog or come up with a technical presentation." The more you do it, the better you'll get at it. Kind of, anyway.

The caveat is that you'll have to find ways of getting feedback; otherwise, you're working in a vacuum. Direct in-person presentations allow you to see the reactions of your audience and the engagement you get from them, and you can reflect on that for the next time. However, when you're building indirect communication skills, you have to find other means of getting that feedback. People might find your content by chance, and they might give you feedback. If they do so, use it to improve. You've got to start somewhere, and it won't be easy, but take advantage of social networks and share your work there. Use your colleagues as guinea pigs, and send your work to them. The topics you cover will most likely be interesting to them as well. Take advantage of places like Reddit, Hacker News, or even Dev.to, where you can reach thousands of developers without having to spend years building an audience. The goal here is to understand the problems you're having when it comes to explaining complex concepts to others and correct them for the next time. Think of it as bug fixing the way you communicate. The more feedback you get and the more you iterate over it, the better it'll be.

Summary

- Work/life balance is crucial to having a healthy career. The more time you spend coding, the less time you'll have to do other things. Avoid burnout by keeping a healthy balance between coding and other aspects of your life.

- You can learn however you want, whether through self-learning on the internet or through more formal education. Either way, what you learn should work toward giving you autonomy in your work. Your focus should also be on becoming better at learning rather than knowing who to ask for help.

- Side projects are great ways of working on your skills, and they also help you create an updated portfolio ready for potential employers. Don't worry how original these projects are. Focus on finishing them and on what you'll learn through the process of building them.

- Open source projects are also a fantastic place to learn about real-life problems, without having an actual job just yet. Consider going through the process of contributing to at least one of them.

- Understand that making mistakes is part of our job—you'll be making mistakes as much as you'll be learning for as long as you're a developer. The point about mistakes is to understand that every problem is a learning opportunity waiting to teach you something.

- Finally, write, write, and then write some more. Keeping a blog as a developer is a must-do if you care about improving your career beyond coding. Writing will give you the practice you need to develop better communication skills through the process of explaining complex concepts in your articles. Remember, developers who can explain themselves are developers everyone wants on their team (trust me on that one).

Interviewing for your place on the team

6

This chapter covers

- How the interview process works
- What to expect from a technical interview
- Things you should and shouldn't say during an interview
- What to expect from a job offer, and how to sort good from bad company perks

Learning a programming language and its associated best practices is only one step on the journey toward getting your first tech job. If you're just starting out, and you're unable to show actual experience for the position you're applying for, a good CV will only take you to the first interview. After that, you're on your own, which is not a bad place to be, but it's important to understand how the interviewing process works and what to expect from it.

Different companies have different hiring processes. Some of them will only perform one interview and make a decision, while others can take up to a month of interviewing and testing. There is no standard, but there are certain patterns of what you'll find and how you should behave (what you should say or avoid saying), which is what we'll tackle in this chapter.

By the end of this chapter, you should understand how the interviewing process works in our industry and some key indicators that will let you know whether a company is right for you or not.

6.1 The tech interview experience

Going for your first technical interview can be nerve-racking if you've never been through a similar process. Actually, scratch that—I've been to quite a few interviews in my 18 year career, and I still get the jitters the day before the interview, so why wouldn't you? After all, we're being evaluated by a complete stranger who doesn't really know us and who has probably not even read our full CV.

The thing you have to remember is that during your interview, you're not just making sure that this person gets to know the "real" you, but you also have to get to know the company and the workplace through that person. This is a two-way interview, even if you weren't told this before.

Let's assume you've applied to your first tech role and have successfully booked an interview. It's for a company you've been eyeing for a while—one that provides services you use daily, and you'd love to work for them. What's your strategy for the interview? Because, yes, you'll need one. Are you planning on saying yes to anything and everything they say? Are you going in with a set idea of what you want, and you won't accept anything less?

Let's cover the basics of what you'll go through and what you can expect from a first technical interview.

6.1.1 What can you expect from a tech interview?

Expectations, expectations, expectations. It's all about expectations. If they're not realistic, your whole experience will be ruined, no matter what you're trying to do. This is why you need to have your expectations grounded before you go into the interview process, especially if it's your first time.

There is no standard when it comes to interviews. Each company will have their own set of practices to follow. Technical interviews usually happen after you have a first personal interview with a human resources (HR) person. They will create a generic profile based on your answers, gather some basic data about you and your experience, and send it to the tech interviewer who will decide whether they want to interview you or not. Some companies, however, will mix both interviews into one and have two (or more) people asking questions and getting to know you, or they'll just go from one session to the next on the same day.

I've had some (although not many) interview processes that lasted for four hours due to them arranging different people to have different types of conversations with me. First I'd get the HR person, then a psychotechnical test would be performed to profile me, and then the actual tech interview would begin. While such long processes aren't the norm, especially now with the possibility of performing the whole thing remotely, they could very well happen to you too.

The entire process is important, but the technical side of it is what makes it unique to developers (all other jobs have a first HR meeting, but none have a tech side like ours), so let's focus on the technical part of the interview. There are different flavors for you to enjoy, and they have their pros and cons. Ask what the process is like, if you have a chance, so you can better prepare for the day.

TECHNICAL CONVERSATIONS

Technical conversations are the ones I always like to have, and this is the way I like to perform the tech interviews myself. In a technical conversation, you'll describe your own experience, highlighting the aspects you feel are most relevant for the position you're applying for, and the interviewer will pick up on keywords and ask you to elaborate on them.

For instance, something I usually do when a candidate mentions they've worked with microservices or APIs is ask if they know what REST is. If they say "Yes," I try to go deeper with "What is considered a RESTful API, then?" So you have to be careful what you say and how you describe your experience. If you make it sound like you're an expert and you barely cover the topic, expect to be asked to explain in more detail.

As part of any job application, we tend to lie or stretch the truth as much as we can. In fact, in 2019 the folks at Blind (www.teamblind.com) ran an anonymous survey of 10,364 developers working for various companies in our industry. Of them, 10% confessed they had lied on their resumes to get their jobs.

Am I telling you to lie on your resume? Of course not. All I'm saying is that just like that 10%, you might be tempted to do so, and lying, especially if you're just getting started, can result in you setting the wrong expectations for the interviewer.

Even lying by omission is a bad practice at this point. For instance, it's common when writing a CV to list a bunch of skills and technologies you're supposed to know. Maybe you're trying to get a frontend developer position, so you list things like these:

- Angular
- React
- Vue.js
- TypeScript
- CSS
- JSX
- Next.js
- Nuxt.js

For a junior role, that's an impressive list of skills. The problem with this approach is that you're playing with the truth. You're not specifying how much you know about each one, so you're leaving your interviewer to assume that part. If they decide to call you because they see this list and think you're an expert on all of these technologies, it's not your fault, is it? Well, it is, kind of.

I get it, it's very tempting to play around with the details and leave parts to be figured out during the interview. After all, you want to get that chance to sit in front of your interviewer and show what you know. Right now it might seem more important to get noticed than to be accurate. But if you go and talk to the interviewer creating these expectations, they'll be very disappointed when they realize the actual skill list looks like this:

- Angular—I've read about it.
- React—I've done a few personal projects.
- Vue.js—I did a to-do app about three months ago.
- TypeScript—I know what it is, but I've never used it.
- CSS—I have a basic understanding.
- JSX—I have a basic understanding.
- Next.js—I've been meaning to try it.
- Nuxt.js—It's the Next.js framework but for Vue.js, isn't it?

When you lie, even if it's by omitting details, the interviewer will expect an unrealistic amount of experience or technical knowledge from you, which will lead to disappointment. And it's not their fault; they're evaluating you based on the fake (or unfinished) profile you presented.

Be up front with your level of understanding of the tech stack. That honesty will pay off. If I see a CV listing a bunch of related technologies without further explanation, I'll be concerned that this person is just adding things to make it look good. However, if they present the same list with their degree of understanding, I'll see them as a developer who's interested in multiple technologies, able to learn on their own and figure out the landscape of their full tech stack. I'll see this person as someone who's willing to learn.

It's common knowledge that recruiters skim through your resume looking for keywords, to see if you might be a fit or not. They even do it on sites like LinkedIn and contact people for jobs using technologies they haven't touched in years (it happens to me a few times every month). The truth is, if your goal is to get the interview, the details won't hurt. Those who skim won't be stopped by those details; they'll just read the keywords you listed, but the interviewer will gain a more accurate understanding of your skills when they review your resume in detail.

To summarize, technical conversations are all about correctly managing expectations. You need to be careful about the way you describe yourself and your experience. Be honest about the things you know and those you don't. Saying "I've never heard about it" or "I've read a bit about it, but I've never tried it" is a lot better than saying "Oh yes, I do it all the time, I just don't remember right now." Lies have short lives, and the less experience you have to cover them, the more obvious they become, so don't lie.

ONSITE TECHNICAL TESTS

Sometimes during an interview, after a short discussion (or none at all), you might be asked to solve a programming problem. They will probably give you a time limit, as well. I personally don't agree with evaluating people in that way, because there is an added stress factor that has nothing to do with the job you're applying for, thus rendering the results (especially negative results) unrealistic. However, declining to do the test will not help you, so while this is a less than desirable situation, you'll have to deal with it.

Some companies will ask you to solve these problems directly on a whiteboard. In these cases you will probably be okay using pseudocode. After all, expecting you to remember a language's syntax by heart is just plain wrong. However, it's also a good idea to state that you used pseudocode to solve it—that way everyone understands that the syntax is just a placeholder.

If, on the other hand, you are asked to perform the test on a computer, there are a couple of options:

- *A testing platform*—There are sites like Coderbyte (https://coderbyte.com/organizations), CoderPad (https://coderpad.io/), and HackerRank (www.hackerrank.com) that provide you with the ability to read a problem, code the solution, and test it against a limited dataset (the full potential dataset remains hidden from you). These problems are usually time limited and have a very narrow set of solutions, often focusing on very theoretical topics, such as understanding how a sorting algorithm works or how data structures such as lists or trees work.
- *A computer with the usual coding tools you'd use at work*—Instead of giving you access to a testing platform, you might be given a computer like the one you'd get if you were to get the job and a problem to solve. These are usually simplified versions of problems the company faces daily, helping them assess more realistically how well you'd do. After all, it makes no sense to test how well you can reverse a linked list (as you would have to do in a testing platform) if you'll never use them in your day-to-day work.

Either of these scenarios could happen with you coding alone or with someone looking at your screen or asking you questions about what you're doing. It's paramount that you understand a few things:

- *It's okay to Google basic things (unless otherwise stated).* Sometimes we tend to get nervous during these types of interviews, and, especially if we're being watched, we think it will look bad if we Google basic things. That's not the case—everyone Googles for help, and it's unrealistic to deem that practice as "bad" or "unworthy of the role." Did you suddenly forget how the syntax of the `for` statement is written? Google it! Or maybe how to pass an attribute as a reference instead of a value? Google it! It's completely fine, and we do it all the time while working.

- *It's not okay to Google the actual solution.* While Googling for help should be allowed, directly Googling the "how to" of the problem you're trying to solve would be crossing the line. You should avoid getting too close to that one and instead focus on Googling only for the related tasks that you don't know how to do or don't remember the exact syntax of.
- *Talk, if the interviewer is there with you.* Do you know what the rubber duck technique is? It consists in using someone (or sometimes, something) to describe your actions. The purpose is to externalize what you're doing as if you were having a dialogue with the duck. Of course, the duck's not going to answer back, and you should not expect your interviewer to give you any meaningful replies either. However, hearing your ideas out loud will sometimes help you spot errors in your logic. This is a great debugging technique used by many developers around the world. I remember having a tinfoil duck on top of my monitor on my first job. My team and I would talk to it anytime we had a problem we couldn't solve. It worked every time.
- *Your interviewer will not help you.* While your interviewer may be there asking you questions, and they may, in some situations, reply to some of your comments, you should not expect them to give you clues as to what you need to do. Don't insist; that looks bad. It's better to accept that you don't know how to do something than to try to get it out of them through questions.

It's hard, but the best thing to do during an onsite technical interview is to try to focus only on the problem you need to solve. Pull from previous experience (if you have any), and try to mentally map this problem to other problems you've solved in the past. This is why working on personal projects while you're looking for your first development job is such a great idea; it gives you this "fake experience" to draw from, which you can use in situations such as this.

REMOTE TECHNICAL TESTS

Some companies will use remote technical tests. In this case, they don't want to know how quickly you can solve a problem; rather, they're looking to get an overall profile of your coding skills.

By giving you a few days and the ability to solve it on your own at home, they're allowing you to get all the help you need, because the fact that you solve the problem is the least important thing for them. Granted, you still need to solve the problem, or you'll most likely fail the interview, but there are other important indicators they'll be looking for:

- Did you add unit tests, even though they never mentioned them? This shows you care about the stability of your code.
- Did you add comments to your code? This shows you care about other people, that you understand you're never going to be working alone, and that others need to understand what you're doing.

- Does your solution take care of edge cases they never mentioned? This shows you pay attention to detail and that you tried to go beyond the initial request.
- Are you following coding standards, whether they're standards provided by the company or from an online source (such as Google or Oracle)? This shows you care about code readability and lets them know you can code as part of a team following the same standard.

Of course, you have to solve the problem, but your focus should also be on these details. That is why you have more time.

On the other hand, here are some practices I would advise against:

- *Delivering sooner than requested*—If they give you three days to solve the problem and you deliver it on day one, chances are you're rushing it, which means you're not really thinking things through. Maybe you're not catching all the potential edge cases, or you've neglected some of the preceding recommendations. Make extra sure that if you're finishing the task considerably sooner than requested, it's not because you're rushing to get the job done.

- *Delivering a lot more than requested*—Going above and beyond the initial request might sound great, but if you go too far you might be showing that you spent very little time on the actual request and a lot more trying to show off. Don't get me wrong. If you play your cards right, this can be a great bonus, but make sure you're able to justify the additions and the time spent on them. For instance, if you're asked to create an API endpoint that pulls data from a third-party service based on a parameter it receives, it's perfectly fine to go the extra mile and add unit tests and maybe schema validation to the request parameters and the response you provide. However, adding a Redis cache to save those results and a React UI to render them is the definition of "too much." You added requirements that aren't trivial to the request, which means you spent a considerable amount of time on them instead of using that time to polish the initial solution. If you want to show your experience and your knowledge, add a "further improvements" document to the deliverable, and explain what else you'd do to this project in order to improve it. But don't go beyond the document—that will show you know more than you've put in your code, but that you focused on the request at hand.

- *Changing some of the requirements*—If you change the language, the framework, or even some of the tasks to solve, you'd better have a very good reason for doing so. The test they're giving you is most likely a simplified version of a task their development team has had to solve in the past, and the overall requirements are there to emulate their working environment. If you change things around, the most likely assumption is that you're not capable of using their tools. If you don't know the framework they're using, or if you've never used the database they ask for, just say so up front and let them know you'll do your best to catch up. That's much better than going off on your own tangent and redefining the test to suit your skills.

No matter the type of technical interview you get, it's not just what you do and say that's important. You should also listen carefully to what your interviewer is telling you about the role and the company culture. You'll potentially be spending quite some time with them, after all.

6.1.2 *Warning signs you should look out for*

The promise of working for a great company should not be the only important factor when deciding to take a job. I know this can be hard to believe when you don't already have a job—in that situation, your first instinct would be to say "yes" to the first available offer. However, passing on an offer that smells funny and then receiving the right one can be worth your while.

In this section, I'll focus less on the technical side of the process and more on the interviewer. I'll give you some clues as to what you should look for in what they say to understand if the job is right for you or not.

BEING A FAMILY IS NOT ACTUALLY A GOOD THING

I've forgotten how many times I've been told by an interviewer how much of a family the company is, and how great a feeling that is for the team. Having a family is great, I get it. You feel like everyone's got your back. I fell for this trap once, but eventually I understood something: companies aren't families, and they can't be.

Let's logically analyze this: if a company works (or feels) like a family, the implications are that

- Everyone will be there to help you when you need it.
- You'll be there for others when they need it.
- You may have a parent-like figure who cares for and looks out for you.
- You should always listen to this figure, because they know better.

Broadly speaking, that turns into

- When the company (the family) needs you, you'll be there for it.
- When you need help from the company (your family), they'll be there for you.
- If you have a question or a request, your boss (your parent) will always be there for you.

That sounds awesome, doesn't it? But there is a catch. Company and government regulations limit the flexibility a company can have regarding its internal policies—policies such as salary bands, study days, sick leaves, and so on. However, there are no regulations limiting your capacity to work extra hours if required, or to sacrifice family dinners for late-night meetings. You can't say "This isn't what I signed up for."

By stating that the company is like a family, these companies are advertising the fact that they might require you to go out on a limb more often than not. You may need to work extra hours to reach a deadline, put on multiple hats (being a developer, a tester, a release manager, and a devops), or make any type of sacrifice for the good of the family. However, when it comes to you needing a favor (something that is implied in a family-like structure), they usually won't be able to help. Need a sick day? You'd better get that doctor's certificate, or they can't prove you're not lying. Want vacation time in the middle of a complicated project? Fine, but stay close to your phone, because they'll reach out if they need you. In essence, while your focus is on them and the project, their focus is on meeting their own deadlines (around projects and revenues) instead of on you.

Companies aren't evil—that's not what I'm saying at all. But you can't think of them as people. There is a lot more going on inside a company than its people, and for a company to stay active and working, executives need to pay attention to those other needs.

This behavior of trying to seem like a family is very common with small startups because they're usually made up of between 5 and 20 people, and everyone knows everyone. The bigger the company is, and the more employees they have, the less it's likely to feel like a family. However, you can still get the same comments from recruiters who are trying to get you to join a team inside a big corporation. The result, though, is the same.

BEWARE OF MANAGERS WHO REMOVE THEMSELVES FROM FAILURES

During the interview process, it is common to be interviewed by your future manager. This allows them to assess how much of a fit you are for their current needs and whether you'll be able to work with the rest of their team. The questions this person will ask are very important, and you should answer them in as much detail as you can, but usually by the end they'll ask if you have any questions yourself. This question is meant to see if you actually care about joining their team and if you've been paying attention to what they've said so far.

This is where you should ask, if they haven't covered the topic yet, about the types of projects they've worked on recently. In theory, you'll ask this because you care about your future assignments, but in reality you'll want the manager to speak about the team's performance. Why? Because the way they do can be very telling.

When a manager shares the wins of their team, they can do it in two main ways:

- *They may include themselves as part of the winning team.* They'll say things like "We completed that project ..." or "We finished that sprint ...." This suggests they share the workload with their team (or they feel like they do), at least when everything turns out for the better. This is important, because it's an indicator that the manager will be there to support their team during the whole process.
- *They may not include themselves on the winning team.* This is also interesting. It means they give 100% of the credit for the success to their teams, and not themselves. They see themselves as facilitators and don't like to take credit for their team's achievements. This is an even better response; it usually shows the manager is not prone to micromanagement and is okay with letting their teams work however they want.

When a manager shares the losses of their team, which you can ask about (for example, "What's the worst project you've been a part of, and why?"), they have the same two options:

- *They may include themselves as part of the losing team.* This is crucial, because it shows how involved they are with their team and that they're humble enough to accept that they're as responsible for the project as anyone else on the team. They could even go one step further and take all the blame, accepting that whatever problems they encountered were due to their not seeing them coming. As facilitators, they should be aware of what's happening and try to troubleshoot before things get worse.

- *They may not include themselves as part of the losing team.* This is not the same as blaming the failure on an external entity (bad client, terrible deadlines, etc.). This is them 100% blaming the team for their mistakes. I've heard things like "Well, the team wasn't senior enough to cope with the workload" or "I got a team that underestimated the effort every time." Trust me, that is a manager you do not want to work for. This is the definition of a manager who's completely fine with throwing their team under the bus to justify their incompetence. Avoid these managers if you can.

Don't let anybody fool you. The interview process is not just for the company to get to know you; it's also for you to get to know the company. By the time you arrive at the interview, all they know about you is what they read on your resume, and you only know about the company what you may have read online or been told by a friend. Both parties need to get to know each other before deciding to work together.

OVERTIME IS NOT MANDATORY, NOR SHOULD IT BE EXPECTED OF YOU

Phrases such as "We work hard and party even harder," or my personal favorite, "We're looking for people willing to show they care about their work, no matter what," usually hide the fact that you'll be working extra hours without getting the extra pay associated with them.

This is highly dependent on where in the world you're working and the company you're working for, but software developers tend to work in a salaried capacity. In other words, you get paid a fixed amount every month under the assumption you work 8 or 9 hours a day (depending on your country). This means that you have a fixed window of time when you should be working, and once that time is over, you're expected to leave.

Sadly, not all companies agree with that. Sometimes the company culture values the project more than anything else, forcing you to either show you agree with them by working extra hours or to be considered the black sheep of the team who cares more about themselves than the group. This is a toxic environment you don't want to work in. Trust me, I've been there.

As an inexperienced developer, you might be convinced that this is the way our industry works: that developers aren't paid for extra hours, and that we need to get the job done, no matter what. I've been there many times. I've seen companies push their employees to that point, and after almost 20 years of it, I can safely say there is nothing wrong with leaving once your shift is over. You and your personal time should be your priority. After all, work is your livelihood, not your life.

Granted, this should be your mantra, but exceptions can be made if you're okay with that. Just remember,

- These should be exceptions, not the rule.
- The decision should be yours, not your manager's or your team's.

I've pulled all-nighters before, due to production deployments gone wrong, or someone thinking that a Friday deployment to production was a good idea, causing the entire team to work over the weekend. But these are exceptions. A continuous overtime policy will only lead to the burnout of the team, which will, in turn, lead to a decrease in their performance, overall bad moods, and eventual attrition, with people leaving the team or even the company.

The next time you have a tech interview, ask about their extra-hours policy. It's perfectly fair that you do so, and if your interviewer considers the question offensive, you have your answer right there. Otherwise, make sure they're clear about it. If they acknowledge that extra hours exist but aren't tracked because "they only happen rarely" or that the company pays for food and drinks when you have to work extra time, you're better off skipping the offer if you can.

With all that said, the perfect job doesn't exist. You'll always find something that you don't agree with in a company. When it comes to extra hours, your best bet is to go with a company that has a clear policy about them. The key word here is "policy." If they have a process for dealing with extra hours, it means they acknowledge that they exist, but it also ensures you'll be treated fairly every time. Mind you, "fairly" can still mean you'll get free food on the weekends, but at least you'll be sure you'll get a free lunch on those days, every time. What you don't want is a vague response—something that is not clear and that could be interpreted in many ways. That's a sign that you'll be pressured into extra hours without any added benefits associated with them.

BEWARE OF UNLIMITED TIME OFF: IT CAN BE A TRAP

The concept of unlimited time off is still relatively new, but it's becoming more common every day. In a nutshell, this means you can take as many vacation days as you like, as long as you complete your goals on time.

On paper, it sounds great. Big companies such as Netflix apply this policy, and employees are in charge of deciding how many days off they take during the year and when. The idea behind it is simple: they know they're hiring responsible adults who can make a conscious decision about when and for how long they can take a vacation. That sounds reasonable, doesn't it? Are you a responsible adult, though?

Answer me this question: when do you think it would be best to take a one-month vacation? Would it be right at the start of a project, so you miss all the starting details and return to an established team as if you were the pariah who decided to ditch them for a summer vacation? Or maybe right in the middle, when things start speeding up and features start going into production? Or heck, maybe right at the end, when the project is closing up and you can show you don't really care how it ends?

Don't worry, you don't have to answer that question. I'm setting you up to show you how our perception of freedom can easily work against us. If we can quickly decide that there is no good moment to take a vacation, then it's easy to assume your manager will think the same way. And if your manager thinks you're being irresponsible for taking advantage of the company's unlimited time off, then when are you going to take it? Never, that's when. Thus it's a "trap."

The same argument could be made for a company that provides regular vacations (such as one or two weeks of paid time off). But in those situations, you're usually forced to take the days off or they expire over time, so this illusion of freedom doesn't exist.

Unlimited time off sounds *AMAZING*, with capital letters, but it needs to be implemented properly. In his book *No Rules Rules*, Netflix's CEO Reed Hasting explains how they arrived at the current iteration of their "unlimited vacations" policy, and he attributes their current success to the inclusion of emotional intelligence into the mix. This means having their leaders take into consideration the emotions and feelings of their teams. It involves measures like these:

- Leading by example and taking vacations themselves
- Avoiding promoting a workaholic culture by rewarding those who never leave or those who put in extra effort every day
- Caring for their team and making sure everyone else is doing the same

Without these measures, instead of giving employees the freedom to rest whenever they're burned out, companies are locking them out of their vacations, making them fearful of being identified as irresponsible or self-centered for leaving when they're most needed. Ironic, isn't it?

The next time you're presented with the option of unlimited vacation in an interview, make sure you ask about it. Ask how the company deals with people who don't take the vacation for fear of being replaced. Ask about their leaders and how often they take vacations. This will show that you've given some thought to the idea and that you're the sort of responsible adult they're looking to give this benefit to. In the end, if the answer you're given doesn't sound right, you may face a mandatory-overtime situation. We covered this scenario in the previous section—it's not a healthy environment to work in, and it's one you should avoid.

6.2   *Things you should never say during a tech interview*

During your interview you'll have plenty of opportunities to talk, either while answering a direct question, or when given the option to talk a bit about yourself, or at the end, when prompted to ask whatever questions you have about the role, the company, or the project. You should definitely speak and be yourself during those moments, but sometimes being too relaxed can be a problem. Not every hiring manager or tech interviewer has your sense of humor (don't I know it!) or will understand your pop culture references. This is why there are some things you should never do or say during a tech interview if you want to create the right impression and show you're the right developer for the job.

Let's take a quick look at my personal top 10 phrases I don't enjoy hearing during a tech interview.

6.2.1   *What do you do here, exactly?*

You may think this question shows you're interested in your interviewer, but in reality you're showing that you didn't come prepared for the interview. These days, and especially in tech, everyone's online. Everyone has an online profile—it can be more or less detailed, but IT professionals will at least have a LinkedIn profile or be listed on their company's website. Take two minutes to Google your interviewer's name (ask whoever set up the interview with you, if you don't already know the name) and cyber-stalk them! Or, you know, find out who they are, what they do, and how long they've been with the company.

It creates a completely different impression if you're asked, "What do you do here exactly?" versus "What's it like to work with Node.js? I read you've been leading teams using that technology for the past three years here." The first question shows mild interest about the interviewer, while the second shows that you did your research and are interested in the work they do.

Of course, going the extra mile here and asking an interviewer you just met, "How's Deborah and the kids? Do they care that you spend 12 hours at work every day?" is too much, and a sign that you did your research a little too well. Keep it professional.

6.2.2   *I don't know, I've never done that before*

As a junior or future developer, you may be tempted to answer some of the technical questions by saying "I don't know." It's true, after all, that you have very little experience, and chances are you'll be asked to solve a problem that you've never encountered.

However, by giving an answer like that, you might as well get up and leave. You've just told your potential new manager that whenever you face an unknown problem, you're blocked and can't solve it. The specific problem with this answer, if you haven't spotted it yet, is that you're not saying what you would try to do. There is a big difference between saying "I don't know" and "I don't know, but I would try to …"

This might sound like a minor distinction, but if you try to reason around the problem with the knowledge you have, you're showing you're capable of adapting and learning. Granted, during your workday you'll usually have access to Google, and you'll be able to use it to research your problems. But take it from someone who's been Googling for almost two decades: Google doesn't have all the answers. Your interviewer knows this as well, so be open to the idea of putting your neurons to work during the interview.

Sometimes asking your interviewer follow-up questions can help you to solve the problem and your interviewer to understand how your problem-solving skills work. For instance, when interviewing data architect candidates, I tend to propose a simple scenario where they have to capture real-time data and store it somewhere to be exploited. If they start asking about time restrictions, tech stack limitations, or available protocols, I can see that they're into it and trying to solve it. Even if they arrive at a solution that is suboptimal, at least I got to see how their problem-solving skills work. This is a lot more valuable than getting, "Well, I've never had to do it, so I don't know. I'd have to Google for an example."

6.2.3 *I hated that place because ...*

One classic question that can pop up during an interview (and which I personally hate being asked) is about your reasons for leaving your current (or previous) workplace. Are you not happy there? Is there a problem, or are you lacking something? Depending on how you feel about your old workplace, this can be a trap, so be careful when answering the question.

If you're looking for a new job and coming from another company, you do not hate the old company (not "officially" anyway). Your previous workplace could have been hell on earth for all I care, but you can't say that. Instead, you should focus on finding the positive aspects of that experience. Maybe say something like, "I feel I've learned all I can from that experience, and I'm ready for new challenges." See where I'm going with this?

Hate is a strong and negative word. You're entitled to feel hatred toward your previous employer, but your potential new employer sitting in front of you doesn't have the full story. If you try to convey what it was like and why you feel that way about the company, all you'll end up doing is showing the worst side of your personality.

Instead, try to focus on what you learned from the previous job and how you tried to turn a challenging situation into a learning experience. That will show that you're a mature adult who doesn't hold a grudge. Is it true? Heck if I know, but it's a great image to transmit to your new manager, so make sure they see that side of you.

6.2.4 *I've built multiple SPAs using SSR with MERN*

Clearly you know your acronyms; just turn them down a notch. The point of the tech interview is to show the person in front of you that you know your stuff, but that doesn't mean memorizing a bunch of acronyms or buzzwords.

Whenever I interview someone, I always start the same way: "If you don't remember a specific term, don't worry about it. Just explain it with your own words." Why do I say that? Because I don't care if the person knows how to say "closure" or "fault tolerant" as long as they can explain those concepts to me using their own words. Anybody can memorize a few words and spit them out during an interview, but if you can explain a concept to me without using those words, then I know you understand it.

6.2.5   *Well, nobody uses that anymore*

This answer can take many forms, but the point is to try to stay away from absolutes. The problem with the phrase here is the "nobody" part. Making a statement in the name of the entire software development industry is a huge endeavor, even for someone who's been part of it for 20 years. Imagine how that might sound coming from a person who's just trying to get into the industry.

Have you heard of COBOL before? It's a programming language that was created in 1959, and it's perfectly fine if you haven't heard about it, because it's currently only used in a few places, like bank mainframes. Or have you heard of Prolog? That's another programming language, but one that's not very popular because it follows a logical programming paradigm instead of following functional, procedural, or even object-oriented paradigms.

Why am I mentioning these languages? Because when they're asked about these technologies, a lot of developers are tempted to say, "Well, that's older than I am; nobody uses COBOL anymore." However, it's not only used, but it's a very sought-after skill because there are very few COBOL developers still around.

This is all to say that absolutes are dangerous because they're either true or false—there are no in-betweens. You're either making a true statement and showing you know your stuff, or you're completely and utterly wrong and showing you don't even realize it (like with the Cobol example). I try to avoid absolutes like the plague, unless I'm 100% sure of what I'm saying (like when I can tell my kids haven't brushed their teeth just by looking at them).

By making absolute statements about the IT industry, all you show is that you're too full of yourself to accept that maybe you don't know everything. That's not a great quality to show during your tech interview.

Instead, try to prepend it with a humble "As far as I understand ..." or maybe a "Last I heard ..." That shows you have an opinion on the matter and at the same time are open to being wrong: a great quality to have.

6.2.6   *It's listed on my resume*

Often during an interview you'll be asked about facts you have on your resume, and especially those you took the time to elaborate and explain. Do not answer these questions with "It's right there on my resume."

Your interviewer isn't lazy. They went over the information you sent, and if they're anything like me, they even tried to dig a bit deeper to verify some of your statements. So why are they asking about something they already read? Because they're giving you a chance to use your own words.

Nobody can tell if you spent 10 minutes or 3 days writing your resume, or even if you wrote it yourself or asked someone else to do it. By answering with your own words, two things will happen:

- The interviewer will know how well you know the topic or how fresh the experience is in your mind.
- During your explanation, you might mention topics that you left out of your resume. This will be a great cue for them to go deeper and ask more about them. One thing I always listen for is the word "microservice" or "API," because they might not be listed as part of the candidate's skills. If I hear them, I'll ask about REST and what that means to the candidate.

Is this a trap? It can be if you don't expect it, but it can also be an opportunity to cover other areas of interest and show you're not a one-dimensional candidate. Imagine having on your resume a personal project you created around Pokemon. It's not a game—it's just a website listing the first 150 Pokemons and their main characteristics (which, by the way, is a very popular first project for people learning web development). On the resume, you'll have listed all the technologies you used, such as Next.js, HTML, CSS, maybe even MongoDB for storage. That yells "web development" to anyone reading it. However, maybe when asked about it, you'll elaborate on the topic and Pokemon and show you've read a thing or two about game mechanics or even game development. Who knows, maybe you've even coded a game or two—this is a great moment to bring that up.

Take these opportunities to add extra flavor to the answer you're giving, and show that there is more to you than what's listed on those pages your interviewer is reading.

6.2.7 *No, I don't have any questions*

When I'm conducting tech interviews, I always like to end by asking the candidate if they have any questions for me. But even if you aren't asked that question, you should try to find a way to ask a few of your own at the end. Remember, this interview is not just for them to get to know you; you need to get to know them too, and the best way to do that is by asking questions.

I'm not suggesting you interview your interviewer, but there are certainly questions you can ask about their role, their job, the type of projects they work on, and the company culture. Saying you don't have any questions suggests you're not really interested in the position, so make sure you at least drop one question before you go.

We've covered a few important questions you can ask in this chapter already. For instance, you can ask about overtime policies, or vacation days and how they are handled. Your question can be as specific as "Do you use scrum or waterfall for your projects?" or as broad as "What's the best part of working here?" This is all useful information that might not come up during the interview but that's important for you to gather before making your decision. So make sure you ask.

6.2.8 *I'm a React developer*

There's nothing wrong with React, but you're selling yourself short with an answer like this. You're not an "[insert tech here] developer," you're "a developer," and there is a huge difference.

Whenever I hear a candidate say something like this, I can't help but put them in a box, because that's what they're doing to themselves. This is one thing you'll have to remember throughout your career: programming is your trade; technologies come and go, paradigms come and go, but the underlying principles remain the same. If you tell me you're an *X* developer, that means you haven't realized this yet. You haven't really understood programming, and you have a lot more to learn.

Instead, be clear that you're "a developer," which means you understand the practice of programming to be something abstract that can be applied to many situations and technologies. This shows you're versatile and willing to learn, which are two major points in your favor. I would pick a candidate like that anytime over a "React expert" who's not willing to switch to AngularJS.

6.2.9   *Oh Linux? I hate Linux, I'm a Windows guy*

There are so many things wrong with this line that I don't know where to begin. But in the context of a tech interview, hating technology is a big no-no.

I get it, I was that guy too. I hated Windows so much I couldn't stand using it for more than 10 minutes. I was a Linux guy for years (macOS guy, if you forced my hand too), but then I understood one tiny detail: it doesn't matter. Tech is a tool, and if you have a choice, you should pick the one that feels more comfortable in your hand (or rather, fingers), but if you don't have a choice, you have to keep moving.

"Hate" is subjective, it comes from a place where reason doesn't exist. Instead, if you think you have a strong argument against the technology, explain yourself: "I haven't had good experiences with Linux when it comes to game development because I've been learning Unity, and the port for Linux is quite unstable." An explanation like this shows you've given it a try and that you're willing to back up your claims with evidence. That's very different—that's not "hating" it, that's experience.

Declining a job offer with great benefits and interesting growth opportunities just because you're not willing to learn a new technology or because you "hate" it only shows you're close-minded. That's harsh, I know, but true. Until you realize that, learning will not be easy, and improving your skills will come at a slower pace. The more tech you try, the more you'll learn—it's that simple. Be open to new opportunities and welcome the unknown; that is the sign of a great developer in training.

6.2.10   *I don't know what unit tests are*

Yes, you're just getting started, but if you don't know what unit tests are, you really haven't learned the basics of programming. I'm not saying don't apply, but maybe stop wasting time on Netflix and read up on the fundamentals of the profession instead.

Why do you think a book like this—one that's not code-focused—dedicates a full chapter to unit tests? Because it is such a fundamental practice in our profession that everyone needs to know it.

Granted, you can't be expected to be an expert unit tester when you're in your first tech interview. There is a lot about the practice that you'll have to learn through experience. However, if you're able to speak about the process, it shows you care about the quality of the code you create. I can't begin to express how valuable that is in a developer, and trust me when I say that not all senior developers care about it that much. If you're looking into unit testing at this stage in your career, you have a great head start.

Finally, there is one last aspect of the interview process that you need to consider: the offering.

6.3 What to expect from the offering after your interview process is over

The last leg of your interview process, after everything's been said and done, is the actual offer. Usually it will come from a human resources professional, and it will come a few days after you've completed the tech interview.

The usual interview process is as follows:

1 You have a quick interview with someone from recruiting, human resources, or even an external psychologist who will create a basic profile about you. The profile will be sent to the tech interviewer to screen.

2 If they deem it interesting, they'll coordinate the tech interview.

3 After the tech interview, they'll send feedback about you to the hiring manager to decide whether or not they make an offer.

There might be other steps between those, depending on the company and how long they think their hiring process should take. But those three basic steps are almost always included.

The first thing you need to do is ask for a few days to study and consider the offer. The company will be expecting a response from you, but you're not obligated to give one right away, especially if the information is conveyed over the phone. This is in no way an attempt to play "hard to get." The point of this time is to weigh the offer against what you have right now. Of course, if this is your first job, chances are you're going to take it, but there are some conditions that can be red flags, so be careful.

If you're just getting started with your career, you can't expect the salary or the overall offer to be great and have all the perks in the world. However, based on what I've covered so far, you should be able to pick up on potential problems with the company or its culture. Don't let the perks disguise a bad offer. Learn to see through them and understand what it really means to work for that company.

6.3.1 Not everything that shines is gold

There are "perks," and then there are "Perks." The problem is that sometimes the former group looks a lot shinier than the latter, so you might end up accepting a sub-par offer because of a few things you can easily get on your own.

For instance, these are classic perks listed in offers that you should really ignore for the time being:

- *Relax zones with ping-pong tables, comfortable couches, and 100-inch flat screens*—That sounds fantastic, but when are you really going to take advantage of that area? When you're working on something, you can't be playing ping-pong or laying on the couch to relieve stress—you need to be working on your deliverable. And if you're currently unassigned because either your project just ended or you've just started working for the company, you'd better be learning something new. Yes, those spaces are awesome for taking five minutes off from your stressful routine and relaxing, but that's all the time you're going to be spending there during your day (or week, really). So don't let that lure you. Understand that while this might sound like a huge perk, it's minor compared to others.

- *Free donut Wednesdays*—I mean, who doesn't like donuts? I love them, and whenever I get one (or as many as I can) for free, you can be sure you'll see me there. That being said, I wouldn't let it be a decisive factor in my decision to take or reject a job offer. I can get donuts on my own just as well, thank you. Substitute donuts for any other type of meal, and you'll have another common perk that's not really a big deal. Free food does not substitute for an increase of 20% on your paycheck, for instance.

- *Working with extremely bright minds*—I'm happy if a team is filled with such individuals, and I will definitely benefit from working with them. However, listing that as a benefit means you're really out of ideas. If your team includes the creators of popular open source frameworks that everyone is using, that's definitely a fact you should drop during the interview, but it's not a perk, and you, as a candidate, should not fall for it. There is no guarantee that any of those "great minds" will have an emotional intelligence high enough to guide you or be a great mentor to you. Good mentors can be found in other places with less "bright" people as well. So let me say this again: this is not a perk, and if you're told it is, you're being mocked.

- *The freedom to travel whenever you want and work from wherever you are*—I was personally offered this perk. I originally thought this person was telling me they flew their employees for things like mass meetups, or something like that. But no, he was just telling me that since I was going to be working remotely, I was free to travel and work from anywhere in the world. "Fantastic," I thought, "I can't really pay rent right now, and this person is telling me I can travel the world. Really?" More and more companies are hiring remote workers these days, and saying that their freedom to work from wherever they want is a "perk" is another big insult, if you ask me. That's not a perk, it's just how "working remote" works. And the worst part? Some companies will list it as a perk, and then once you join will tell you that it's dependent on the project, and if the client doesn't want you to be in the wrong time zone, you can't do it.

I could keep listing examples, but you get the point. A perk is not anything other than your salary. Instead, it should be something that really benefits you. Perks are what the company offers to lure you to work for them. However, perks need to be useful to you.

6.3.2 *Actually useful perks*

This list could also be endless, because it's up to the company's imagination what they offer. However, let's cover a few that I've seen in my years of jumping between companies:

- *Flexible hours*—Real flexible hours mean you work whenever you can (or want), as long as you either deliver your work on time or complete the allotted working hours every day. This is usually a perk for remote workers, and it's great because it allows you to organize your work around your daily routine. For instance, I used to be able to take my kids to school every morning, and I would start working after that. I would work until it was time to pick them up, and I would do so with my wife. I was part of their routine, even though I was working from home. I really enjoyed that flexibility and that time with them. That's an actual perk.
- *Company gear*—A laptop, and probably a phone if you're expected to travel, are usual perks that most tech companies offer their employees. This is a fairly standard perk, and it's great because you shouldn't be expected to buy your own gear. Not when you're going to use it to create intellectual property (the software you'll write) that's not yours.
- *Paid parental leave*—This is a real perk that more and more companies are starting to offer. Having a child is no easy task, and even if you're not the mother, you'll still need time to be there for everyone, so having paid parental leave (whether you're the mother or the father) is a great opportunity. In my case, when my first kid was born, I had three days off paid by the company—that was it. I had to take all my pending vacation days so I could take two weeks off to be home with them. Did I regret not having vacations that year? Heck no, but if your company is capable of acknowledging that you'll need the time off, that's a much better deal.
- *On-site, free gyms*—Working as a developer is a very sedentary profession, and we tend to spend most of our days sitting in the same exact position. But we're humans (no matter how much we'd like to deny that fact), and we need physical activity. The problem is that sometimes we don't have enough time, especially if we have long commute hours. This is why on-site gyms are a great opportunity to get some exercise over lunch time or even after work. Having the gym right there for free removes every single excuse for avoiding it. Companies like Google are starting to implement this in all their offices. It shows they care about their employees' health. A perk that benefits your health? Yes please!

Notice how I didn't mention anything about free meals or relax rooms in that list. That's because actual perks try to benefit your work/life balance by giving you time off when you need it (like when a new baby is born) or helping you improve the way you live. Perks aren't about giving stuff for free, but rather about companies showing their employees they care about them.

The next time you receive an offer from a company with a sub-par monetary offer, check out their perks and consider what you've learned here. Maybe that company isn't worth your while, or maybe they are, and the low salary can be compensated for by the great perks. In the end, only you know what your dream job is and what's most important to you. So ask yourself the following questions (or similar ones that matter to you):

- Where do I see myself in five years? Can I get there with this job? Or is this job a starting point to get there eventually?
- What's the most important thing for me right now? Is it money? Freedom to work from home? Making my own work schedule?
- Do I want to work for a big company where I'm one of many, or do I want to go through the startup experience and be part of a small group of developers doing everything themselves?

If you think your answers are compatible with the offer, then you've got your "Yes!" Otherwise, it should be a "Thanks, but no thanks," and you can keep on looking.

Summary

- The interview process is not only meant for the company to get to know you. It's also a great opportunity for you to get to know them, so make sure you ask questions and get all the details you need to make an informed decision.
- Don't lie during the interview or in your resume. Lies have very short lives, and they only help to create wrong expectations about you. Try to show your worth through other means. If you don't have any, then it might be a sign that you're not doing enough.
- Be careful what you say during the interview. Showing interest about things you can't possibly know, like their day-to-day tasks and company culture, is a great idea. Asking about obvious or easy-to-find information shows you haven't done your homework.
- Try to stay away from absolute statements. You probably lack the experience to back them up, and that's perfectly fine. There is nothing wrong with giving your opinion about a subject; just make sure it's clear that you're basing it on your limited experience.
- Watch out for classic red flags like improperly implemented unlimited time off, mandatory overtime, and managers who won't share the burden of a failed project with their teams.
- Finally, not every perk is worth your time, and you need to sort the good ones from the easy and not really useful ones. Remember, flexible work hours are fantastic, but free donuts shouldn't be considered a perk.

Working as part of a team

You are never alone as a developer, even if right now you're working on your first project by yourself in a dark room. That code may be intended as part of your portfolio, or perhaps it's a new product you're hoping to release, but the moment you need advice or help from others, you'll stop being alone. It's just a matter of time.

No matter how much you try to work on everything alone, you'll soon realize that there is a lot more to a software project than just the code. And you know what? That's good! Accepting that you'll never be alone is the perfect first step to start learning how to be a good team player, because sooner or later you'll be working as part of a larger team. If you don't know what that means for you, the whole experience will go as smoothly as swallowing a smoothie made from rocks. This chapter will outline the social and technical tools you need to make that first team experience a success.

7.1 Getting your manager to love you

The development team you're going to be a part of is not only composed of other coders like you; it'll have multiple roles, and one that you'll want to pay special attention to is your manager.

Suppose you're starting your very first job as a developer. You're introduced to your team and your project, and now you're starting to deal with your manager. You quickly figure out that one potential way up in your team is with the help of your manager. You just have to impress them—take their breath away, if you will. So what can you do, other than kicking them right in the gut when they're least expecting it? (Please note that this is intended as a joke. The author of this book does not condone kicking your manager in the gut for any reason—especially your current manager.)

Let's look at some options that will help you achieve this without raising many strange questions.

7.1.1 Task-tracking software is not the devil's tool

Task tracking is not evil, even when sometimes it might feel like it is. I know, we all want to code and forget about the world for eight hours straight, but that's not only impossible, it's impractical as well. Coding is going to be your main task during your work iterations, and it's definitely going to be your focus. It just can't be your only focus. Task tracking is one of those noncoding activities developers tend to either hate or underestimate to the point where they'll leave it to the very last day.

The first thing to understand is that task tracking is not meant for you. You already know what you're doing, and if you are somewhat organized, you also know what pending work you have. So why does your manager keep asking you to update the task-tracking tool every day?

Put yourself in the shoes of your manager. You have a team of developers working on the next release of a feature. You've made a commitment to the stakeholders (be it the company owner, a potential outside client, or any other person who has a stake in this release), they are counting on you to meet the deadlines, and they're basing their business strategy around that fact. On the other side, you have your team, wailing at their keyboards, trying to finish the feature on time.

When your stakeholders call to see how everything is going (because they will), how will you answer them? Your job as a manager is to always understand how the project is going and to know if there are any blockers or delays and why. To get that information, you have three options:

- *Assume*—You assume your team is doing the best they can and that everything is going smoothly, because, otherwise, they would have said something. Of course, this is *completely wrong*. Not all developers will say something when there is a problem, and if their initial estimates are wrong and the task is too complex to finish on time, you'll never know until it's too late.

- *Ask repeatedly*—You go one by one, having a quick talk with every developer, asking for a status update. This will take between 10 and 30 minutes per developer (depending on the task and the developer). In an 8-hour work day, 30 minutes doesn't sound like a lot, does it? Wrong, it *is* because you're not just taking 30 minutes of their time; you're breaking their concentration and asking them to switch mental contexts. That is, by itself, a huge effort, and it'll take them more time to get back into the flow they were in before your interruption. And to top it all off, you have to take notes and then summarize them to produce some sort of overall report.

- *Track*—Get the information from a summary report produced by the task-tracking tool you and your team are actively using. Yes, this is absolutely the right way to do it. Of course, this can only work if your team is actively updating the tool, which is why you have to remind them, every day if it's necessary, that they need to do it.

Step out of your manager's shoes now and back into your own. Is your manager still pesky and annoying? Or are they only trying to do their job, and you're not really helping? A quick status update can be as simple as dragging a card from the To-Do column to the In Progress column. Or it can mean entering a comment mentioning that you've hit a blocker, or perhaps adding, at the end of the day, the approximate number of hours you've worked on a task. It takes you a minute to do, and your manager will love you for it.

Let's take a look at another area where you'll need to focus: meetings.

7.1.2 Meetings!

Meetings are feared and loathed by many developers because they see them as a big waste of time. In fact, you can even get T-shirts on Amazon that say "I survived another meeting that should've been an email." I'm not saying developers coined the phrase, but it's definitely a common catchphrase in our industry. Whose fault is it, though? And are all meetings unnecessary and a big waste of time?

No, they're not, especially now that remote work is becoming the norm for some companies. Meetings are required, and a well-organized and -executed meeting can provide a lot of value. The key is to focus on the meeting's purpose and try to keep the conversation on topic the whole time.

As a developer, you're expected to join multiple types of meetings:

- *Status updates*—Usually you'll have to join a quick call with the whole team (unless the team is big enough that it merits submeetings) every day. This meeting is supposed to end quickly, and you usually need to speak about your tasks from the day before, any potential blockers you may have, and the tasks you'll be working on that day. This is known as "daily standup" in practices such as scrum or agile, because it happens daily, and it's meant to be performed while standing up, so everyone will hurry up with their updates. Other methodologies may implement variations on this daily status update. The point is that you'll likely have meetings of this sort.

- *Ad hoc meetings to resolve a blocker or answer a question*—These meetings will usually involve you and whoever can give you the solution you need. You'll have to prepare for these meetings by being capable of explaining what you need and why.

- *Demo meetings*—If you're working on a product, you'll usually have to join demo meetings to help answer any specific technical questions about the feature you worked on, or perhaps to show what you've done and how it works. Depending on your project, your team's composition, and the way your project is handled, you might not be required in these meetings, especially if you're just getting started. Eventually, though, you'll be joining them as well.

- *Retrospective or postmortem meetings*—These may be called something else where you work, but the point of these meetings is to review past work, understand what went well so you can double down on it, and what went wrong so you can try to fix it for the next work iteration. These meetings are usually less technical and more social in nature, but their focus is still your project and your work, so don't be fooled by the lack of tech jargon. Some teams tend to ignore these meetings and power through any issues they might be having. That's not ideal, and if you find you're seeing a lot of problems and not having an opportunity to discuss them, it might be a good idea to bring this type of meeting to the attention of your manager.

There may also be other meetings where you work; it's really up to your team and your manager. However, there is one consistent characteristic about all of them: they're meant to serve a purpose. Notice how I said "meant to." If the participants do not take the meeting and everyone else's time seriously, the purpose might be lost, so consider meeting etiquette important when joining one (either in person or online):

- *Be there on time.* That doesn't mean joining the call or getting to the meeting room exactly when the meeting is supposed to start. Being there on time means arriving or joining a few minutes early. That way you're ready to get started when the meeting starts. Joining at the moment the meeting starts means being late, because people will say "Hi" to everyone and you'll all lose a few minutes from the meeting. The more social you'd like to be, the sooner you should be there so you avoid wasting the time of those arriving closer to the starting time.

- *Avoid chitchat during the meeting.* Whether it's an online or in-person meeting, remember that you're all there for a reason. Unless this is a social meeting, you have a limited window of time to cover the topic (or topics) at hand. Chitchatting or having small conversations in the middle of discussing a topic will only delay the meeting and waste everyone's time. If you join a few minutes early, you can catch up with people before the meeting starts without interrupting anyone.

- *Prepare for the meeting, don't just "wing it."* The best way to take advantage of a meeting is to show up prepared. If you're going to ask questions, have them already written down. If you're demoing something, make sure everything works and that you've done a predemo meeting to practice. If you're presenting a complex idea, try to have a presentation that you can share, so others don't have to follow your explanation to understand it. With proper preparation, you'll avoid having dead time while you figure things out.

- *Make sure there are actionable items at the end of the meeting.* This may be optional, depending on the meeting type, but if you're trying to solve blockers, ask for requirements, or identify things you or someone else will need to take care of, summarize them at the end. This will help people with tasks to remember them and make sure they understand what the next step is. Through this practice, you're can also plan the next step in the process you're going through. If you skip this step, the meeting might end with everyone going back to their usual tasks without knowing what they have to do next. If that happens, the meeting was, indeed, a waste of everyone's time.

- *Align with everyone in the meeting by sending the meeting's minutes afterwards.* The minutes of the meeting should summarize what was discussed:
  - Who joined the meeting? List all joiners by name.
  - What points were discussed? Bullet points will be enough; just make sure you capture every topic covered.
  - Were decisions made during the meeting? If so, list them here as well.
  - Action items. This goes hand in hand with my previous point. If at the end of the meeting people left with homework, list those items here and who is responsible for each item.

  By sending the minutes via email, you'll make sure that everyone is aligned on the outcome of the meeting, giving them the option to speak up otherwise. If there were misunderstandings, and nobody noticed them, your minutes will highlight them. Without minutes, if those misunderstandings, cause problems, it'll be your word against theirs, and that is never a good way to solve a problem.

Some of these activities might not be your responsibility at the beginning, especially if your manager is involved in the meeting. But your manager won't always be there, and by showing you know how to get the most out of meetings, you'll show your manager you are organized, respectful of others' time, and action-oriented—three sought-after qualities for any developer.

That leads me to another ability every developer needs to develop over time: planning.

7.1.3   *I plan, therefore I code*

Coding may be second nature to you. Maybe you're used to thinking through a problem while writing the code that solves it. Perhaps that has worked for you so far, because there is one key thing you probably haven't had to do until now: estimate your work.

Estimating their work is a skill that most software developers are lacking when starting their first job. This is completely expected, since the ability to estimate comes from experience, and you have none (or close to none). And to your dismay, this is one of the things every manager will ask you about. They might help you in the beginning, if they know a thing or two about what you need to do, or maybe one of your more experienced colleagues might jump in and provide some guidance. That will be fine at first, but you'll have to start understanding how to provide this information yourself. Being able to estimate your work shows experience—it shows mileage, if you will; the inability to do so shows you're new and inexperienced. Being new and inexperienced is perfectly fine, but not being able to estimate your work a year after you've started working as a developer is a big sign of problems.

Now keep in mind that estimations will always be wrong. I'll let you in on a little industry secret: estimating is not about getting the number right, it's rather about who gets the closest number. You can't predict life. You might be trying to estimate a task that you've done 100 times already, but the minute something doesn't go according to plan (a family emergency may force you to take a few days off, there may be a missing external dependency, etc.) your whole estimate is no longer valid. While your estimates can become quite accurate over time, it's unrealistic to ask a junior developer to provide accurate estimations. What can you do, then, to solve that problem?

Plan your work. Stop your irresistible urge to code for a little longer, and grab a piece of paper and a pen and start writing, drawing boxes, or whatever necessary to somehow lay down a plan for your work. Try to estimate everything you'll have to do. Don't worry about the time right now, and just focus on breaking down the big task into smaller chunks—sub-goals, if you will.

For example, imagine the task says "Create the login page for users of the application with React" (React being a JavaScript framework used for UI development). Start by breaking it down into steps like these:

1 Create the React component to hold the code that interacts with the backend service used to verify credentials.
2 Write the HTML for the page.
3 Create the CSS for the page to mimic the design.
4 Insert the new component into the routing configuration of the application.
5 Visually test that the component looks right.
6 Test if the component is interacting with the service properly.

I could go on, but you get the point. I went from a single directive to six smaller ones. Can you now estimate those? Are there some that you still don't know how long they will take you? If so, keep breaking those up into even smaller chunks. The trick here is to keep breaking down the complex tasks until you're able to estimate, and then start adding up those numbers. You can probably create a table like table 7.1 to review your estimates.

Table 7.1 The final estimate numbers

Task	Estimate (in hours)
Create the React component to hold the code that interacts with the backend service used to verify credentials.	12
Write the HTML for the page.	4
Create the CSS for the page to mimic the design.	4
Insert the new component into the routing configuration of the application.	1
Visually test that the component looks right.	0.5
Test if the component is interacting with the service properly.	1
Total estimate	**22.5**

You went from not knowing how to estimate your work to having a reasonable number: 22.5 hours. This translates to almost 3 days of work (assuming 8 full hours of work every day). You can use 3 days as your estimate, instead of saying 22.5 hours, because it's more realistic and adds a small buffer for dealing with things like coffee breaks and the occasional distraction.

Being able to provide this estimate, even if in the end it is off by 2 days, is a great start, and it'll look great in the eyes of your manager. It shows you're capable of analytical thinking, and you're showing that you're basing your decisions on logic instead of picking random numbers.

I know the preceding example is simplistic. Maybe your tasks are so complex that they'll take a few hours to split into manageable chunks. That's fine. This is an exercise you'll be doing for a while, but with time you'll start seeing repeating patterns. Maybe you won't have to create a login form next time, but you'll have to create a contact form. You've already built a similar component, so you'll only need to focus on the differences to come up with an estimate for the new task. It'll be faster, and because it's based on past experience, it'll be much more accurate.

Over time you'll be able to estimate whole sprints or even several months of work and eventually a full project. Granted, the bigger the estimate, the more error prone it'll be, but there's another trick you can use when you think you're a bit over your head: use assumptions.

When you're estimating a big chunk of work, you'll sometimes see holes in your plan. There are things you don't know or that you'll have to research to understand. In this situation, one option is to make an assumption about what that section of your plan will look like, and then carry on with your estimate. Instead of doing that, though, you can write a note about each assumption you make during the process. That way you can go to your manager and show them your final number, but you can also point to the list of things that need to happen in the right way (your assumptions) for your estimate to work.

Going back to the example in table 7.1, you're making the assumption that the backend service for validating credentials is already working, but what if it isn't? And for the CSS task, you're assuming you'll have a finished design by the time you start this part of the work, but what if it's not there? Add those assumptions to your list. Mark them as dependencies, and make sure that your manager is aware of this.

By going through this estimating process, you've not only created a reasonable estimate without having a lot of experience, you've also highlighted *dependencies* and *risks*. You're on fire! That is pure value added, and, trust me, not a lot of developers know to do that. Instead, they'll silently assume the best scenario for their estimates, and they'll see it all burn to ashes when the dependencies aren't met.

7.1.4 *Don't reinvent the wheel*

Just because you can develop some functionality doesn't mean you necessarily have to. This is highly dependent on your field of work, but unless you're the very first developer trying to do something within that field, others have probably created libraries and published reusable lines of code somewhere for you to take advantage of. With that in mind, why would you want to recode a piece of logic yourself?

Going back to our login-related example, imagine you're tasked to create the login logic on the backend, so your users can use their Google account to sign in. That is called single sign-on (SSO), and it's been done to death in every possible language. So what do you think would be the right approach here?

- Take this opportunity to read up on how SSO works, and implement the mechanics yourself.
- Consider the project's timeline and use one of the recommended libraries.

You don't have to be a retired cold-war spy to read between the lines and figure out what my suggestion would be, do you?

While learning how things work is a major part of your career development, you can do so on your own time or in smaller chunks with guided help during the development of a feature. Going all in and fully implementing a solution just so that you can learn how it works shows you're not taking into consideration the quality and timeline of your project. I'm not saying you'd be doing this on purpose, but it is the message you are sending your manager. Going with the tried and tested library will save time on one hand and ensure the quality of your work on the other.

When is a good idea to reinvent the proverbial wheel? Reusing external libraries is definitely the way to go in most situations, but there might be times when it's perfectly okay to re-implement someone else's function. Some companies or projects require you to avoid having external dependencies, because you don't have direct control over them. If, for example, the feature you're working on is core to your product, and you're basing it on a third-party library, you're running a huge risk if its owners decide to stop maintaining it. Or perhaps they have a roadmap that is not aligned with the features you need to develop in the future. There are many reasons why having your own implementation makes sense.

Another reason is security. In 2018 the owner of a very popular npm repository was running out of time to maintain it, so he gave it away. Little did he know that the person who offered to take care of it was a hacker who went on to add malicious code and release a new version. Every project that depended on that library and had not frozen the version they depended on received the new update and started leaking private information. The library in question was called `copay-dash`, and while you can still install it, you'll get a deprecation warning stating: "npm WARN deprecated copay-dash@2.4.0: This package is deprecated, and has a unfixed event-steam vuln. Do not use."

Given that, you can probably understand why some developers might want to avoid depending on external libraries. This type of security issue is not that common, though, and writing all your own code will considerably increase your project's timeline just because of a "what if" scenario. This type of problem can also be avoided in many ways, such as by locking a version of the library in your dependency definitions so you're not surprised by new updates.

Don't get me wrong, this is a big issue when it happens. Allowing malicious code to run on your servers can have catastrophic consequences. However, there are less dramatic ways of avoiding this problem than taking a full start-from-scratch approach.

In the eyes of your manager, being able to understand the impact your decisions have on the timeline is already a huge deal. If you can decide whether or not to reimplement something based on logical and well-founded reasoning, you'll gain a few extra points right there.

7.1.5 *What you should never say to your manager*

Let me begin by stating that I'm a firm believer that your work should speak for you when it comes to your managers. Through the work you do, they should be able to understand if you're adding value to the team or the company overall.

With that out of the way, I think it's also important to understand the types of messages we might be indirectly transmitting through our behavior—not necessarily through the actual tasks we close or the solutions we come up with, but rather through the way we handle everything around our work. After all, while our work can be very important to us, we're also going to have to deal with other personal activities and priorities. The way we handle them, and the way we let them affect (or not affect) our interactions with our team, will also show a great deal to our managers.

We could cover this from many perspectives, but here I want to look at this form of communication from the point of view of a manager. I want you to learn how to read between the lines of the classic excuses and justifications we tend to use, and to understand why they're not the best thing to say.

Note that this is not meant to be a cheat sheet on how to come up with valid excuses. This section will demonstrate that in some situations, it's better to understand the impact you had on your team and to accept the penalty (whatever that might be) than to try to justify your actions with an excuse that will actually make things a lot worse.

SORRY I'M LATE, I WENT OUT PARTYING LAST NIGHT

I've heard this one, multiple times, and I personally don't understand it. Maybe it's because I'm not the partying kind, but I tend to believe that life and work should not mix, and this means that whatever you do in your spare time should not affect your work or your performance at work.

Don't get me wrong, your personal life always needs to be more important than work. And if you do happen to have an emergency, I would argue you're more than justified to come in late, or even not come in at all. However, if you're coming in late with the excuse of a party or a late hang-out with friends, you're telling me that you don't care enough about the project to show up on time. Not only that, but you're also saying you don't really care about or are oblivious to the effect your actions have on others. Your team will have had to pick up the slack while you weren't there, and don't even get me started if it was a deployment day or if you missed an important meeting.

I know, that sounds a bit harsh, and I'm not here to be your dad. I'm just explaining how others might read the message you'd be sending—even if you're late because it was your brother's 18th birthday. Think about the message you're sending.

In moments like these, an excuse is probably the worst thing you can give, especially if you're not asked for one directly. Own up to your mistake, appreciate your team, and accept that what you did to them was not ideal. That will show your manager that you're mature enough to be aware of what you're doing and that your actions have consequences. That might sound like a given to you, but trust me, this amount of common sense is not exactly ... common.

BUT WE'VE ALWAYS DONE IT LIKE THAT

Imagine saying that to your manager when you're presented with a bug. Just because you have a predefined way of working, and it's been successful until now, it doesn't mean it's fail-proof. Being this closed-minded to change can send the wrong message.

Every time you receive a bug report, you should review it, even if it goes against everything you know (or think you do). Even seemingly perfect systems might have some hidden flaws, and you won't find them by blindly trusting the creation of another developer. No system is perfect, and every bug report, no matter how crazy it might sound, needs to be reviewed, checked, and confirmed before disregarding it as "not valid."

Saying a bug report is "not valid" as a reflex response is the sign of a closed-minded developer. Saying "Let me review it and I'll get back to you," shows an open-minded individual ready to learn and grow. That's the image you want your manager to see and the message you want them to receive.

NOT MY FAULT!

When a problem arises, it affects all team members. Even if you're not directly responsible for the problem, saying "not my fault" shows you don't really feel you're part of that team. At least, that's the message you're sending.

Instead, there are many ways you can help someone solve the problem. You can help them troubleshoot and find the cause of the issue, or you can help them debug the issue. Even if you're a frontend developer and the problem is in the backend, or vice versa, chances are you have some kind of value to add or ideas to share. It's all code, after all!

In the worst case scenario, you can be their rubber duck—I discussed this idea in chapter 6 (section 6.1.1). The "rubber duck" term comes from a famous technical book called *The Pragmatic Programmer*, by Andrew Hunt and David Thomas (Addison Wesley, 1999), in which the authors told a story about a developer carrying around a rubber duck and using it to debug his code by explaining his ideas to the duck. Of course, the duck is merely anecdotal in the story, since the real power comes from the actions of the developer. By explaining things out loud, he was able to hear himself and his ideas and look at them from an outside perspective.

That's the key. Have you ever thought you had a great idea until the minute you spoke it out loud and realized it was terrible? That's the power of this technique. Whenever you come up with an idea and don't run it by anyone, you create assumptions about it, and your solution becomes biased by them. By externalizing these ideas, even if it's just with a rubber duck, you're able to hear the bias and course-correct your solution.

This is essentially the long way around to saying that even if you're not capable of helping by coding the actual solution, you can still help.

Whew, that's a lot of work!

Do not complain about work being too hard. That's it, that's the advice.

Alright, I'll try to elaborate a bit here. You may now be in a position where you've got everything handled, you know exactly what you have to do, and you know how you're going to do it. That's your comfort zone, and that's a terrible place to be. If you get assigned a new, harder task, and you immediately complain about the work that it represents, you're showing you're not willing to learn. You're showing rigidity. This is not only bad because of the way it looks, it's terrible for your own professional growth. You're literally fighting to stay inside your comfort zone where you don't do anything new. You might be the best at what you do, but you'll never be good at anything else. Getting new work is not a reason to complain; quite the opposite, it's an excuse to learn something new. That's how you grow.

Every time you sigh about your assignment, your manager is going to make a mental note: "He's not happy about doing this." If this keeps on happening, eventually there won't be any new work you're actually excited to do. Can you imagine what that would look like?

Instead of sighing and complaining, accept that you'll often be faced with unknown tasks and that figuring them out is part of the job. There's no way around it.

I'm bored, I don't know what to work on

Never tell whoever is managing you that you're bored. That single word has a lot of negative connotations—it tells everyone that you lack proactivity, you find yourself without work, and suddenly you stop, you freeze. That's not the right attitude. Raise your hand and explain that you've run out of work and you're open for new tasks—that's a very proactive attitude. Or find a way to create your own tasks, as long as they're relevant and don't go against your current work iteration. Be proactive; that's the key takeaway from this point. Proactive is good, whereas reactive (waiting until others tell you exactly what to do) is bad.

Mind you, you can get bored even if you do have tasks to work on. It's important to accept that you won't always like what you have to do. Sometimes the task ahead seems boring as heck, and you have no way to avoid it. You'll always have two choices when confronted with one of those tasks:

- You can be miserable and do it anyway. Get the job done, and move on to the next task.
- Find an interesting way to take on the task (maybe find a new framework you've never used before, or a new scripting language you've been dying to try).

Both options yield the same result for the outside observer (your manager), but I like the second option a lot more. With that option, I'm not only getting the job done, I'm also learning something new while doing it. Win-win!

IT'S A RANDOM BUG

We covered the random bug mystery in section 2.4, but it's such a common excuse that I thought I'd mention it again. Computers are not random, so bugs can't be random either. You have to learn to use root cause analysis to determine the causes.

But that's not what I want to discuss here. I want to cover the other side of the coin: not how to solve a "random bug" but why believing that a bug can be random sends the wrong message to your manager. Declaring a bug as random shows two things about you:

- You believe the product is not important enough to merit your time debugging it. With that approach, the root cause, and the solution, are not going to be found anytime soon.
- You're accepting that the user, your most important stakeholder, will have to deal with this problem from time to time.

Neither of those messages is good.

Instead, see this bug as an opportunity. Finding a potential solution is not enough; you also have to understand exactly what's causing the problem and find a way to ensure that it never happens again. This is the attitude you want your manager to see: a proactive developer (I've mentioned proactivity before, haven't I?) who worries about the quality of the product. This shows you're committed, and that's the right message to send.

We've now covered the attitude you need to make your manager happy and show you care. Let's move on to your team next.

7.2 *Being a good teammate*

We've talked about your manager, so let's focus on your team now—all those other developers and non-developers who are there working with you to get the project ready for production.

If you're reading this while working on your first job, you may be wondering what the point of this section is. "Why do I need to be a good teammate? How does this make me a better programmer? I just open my laptop, write some code, and at the end of the day I'm out. I don't need to interact with anyone for that." With that in mind, let me give you the TL;DR version: you're wrong. Let's elaborate.

7.2.1 *Make peace with your testers*

Just like cats and dogs, the idea of developers getting along with their testers seems unnatural for some reason, which is crazy if you think about it. They are two sides of the same coin—why would they have to hate each other? There's no reason. This might sound obvious, but it took me years to reach that realization, and that's a bit embarrassing, to be honest.

Why wouldn't you hate them? They're constantly finding defects and problems with your logic and with how you build the product. They're making you look bad. That's usually what goes through developers' heads, but it couldn't be further from the truth. Testers are responsible for their own piece of the software development life-cycle, the testing part. Figure 7.1 shows the full cycle, but step 5 is highlighted, which is where the testers' involvement is most relevant.

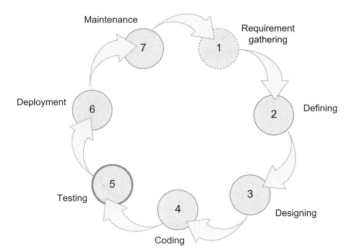

Figure 7.1   The software development lifecycle

There are seven steps in the software development life cycle:

1 *Requirement gathering*—This is where you listen to your client and understand what they want.

2 *Defining*—This is where you and your client settle on the product to be built, based on the requirements you gathered.

3 *Designing*—Before writing any code, you need to have an idea of what you're going to be building. This phase is not only about UI design, but about overall architecture as well.

4 *Coding*—Now we're talking. This is where we write the code that makes everything defined so far a reality.

5 *Testing*—This is the validation of the coding work. This is where the quality threshold is set, and if your work does not meet that threshold, it won't move forward.

6 *Deployment*—Here you move the tested work into the hands of the users.

7 *Maintenance*—When your deployed code is no longer going to be heavily changed, you might keep adding to it or fixing small problems, but the overall feature is done.

Those are not absolute steps, and every project will go through them multiple times, which is why it's a cycle and not a straight path from start to finish.

Of these, step 5 is where our work, which we deem ready, is validated by the actual experts. We can't do it ourselves—we're too biased. We built it, after all, and just like parents will shout to the seven winds that their kids are the most beautiful in creation (even when they're not), we can't see the problems with our own code. The true test of quality comes from the validation of an objective party: the testing team, sometimes also known as the *quality assurance* team or the *quality control* team.

What if they end up finding problems or bugs in your work? That's fantastic! I know, I know, you wanted to close the task and move on to the next one. But consider the alternative—those problems would have been found by the users instead. That's not a thing you want to happen.

Imagine being a tester who's handed a feature that, according to the developer, is "ready for production," only to find out, based on the requirements that originated the feature, that only 3 of the 10 requirements listed are indeed ready. That would be frustrating, wouldn't it? Now imagine going through that process several times a day. Learn to appreciate the work of others, even if they don't write code for a living. If they're part of your team, that means they have a role to play, and it's just as important and as relevant as yours.

The moment you start getting along with your testers and taking their work seriously, you'll start seeing your productivity increase. You'll deliver fewer faulty features because you'll know what they usually look for, and you'll be able to fix those before moving the code to their testing environment. Remember, testers are not out to get you. They're actually there to stop you from screwing up in front of everyone, so appreciate them and treat them with the respect they deserve.

7.2.2   *Leave your ego at the door*

I'm a firm believer that ego is a part of us all, as humans, but developers tend to have this particular trait overdeveloped. I think that's because, as developers, we're creators, small-scale gods, at least when things work out the way we want them to. We tell these cold, lifeless machines what to do and how to do it. And if we practice enough, that can take the shape of a 3D game or a new algorithm that can detect cancer early on, or it can potentially even mimic human intelligence. With enough time and grit, we can do anything, and that sensation is intoxicating.

As we grow in knowledge and understanding, our egos can grow out of proportion. But as you've probably realized by now, the best developers are the ones who recognize that they'll always have something new to learn, and that can't happen with an ego that's out of control.

This is why developers with huge egos are effectively shouting to the world that they're really inexperienced children playing grown-up. Note that I'm not using the word "experience" here to refer to the amount of time they've worked in the industry. Instead I'm referring to life experience, which definitely takes years into account, but also lessons learned and the wisdom that comes with them. This is all to say that you can have developers who have worked for 10 years but are still inexperienced enough to run around with their egos unchecked. It's a phase we all go through, but it's also important that we learn enough to outgrow it.

Let's look at several symptoms that can help you identify this problem, both in you and in others.

YOU THINK YOU KNOW EVERYTHING

You don't. No really, I'm not guessing here, you don't. I'm 100% sure of it.

The key is that you realize it too, and sometimes that's not straightforward. You know what happens if you consider that you know everything about a topic? Two very bad things:

- You close your mind to others teaching you or correcting you when you're making a mistake. That means you'll be screwing up, and you won't even recognize help from others.
- You're officially done learning about the topic at hand, because, after all, you know everything about it. So you're making the conscious decision to not look for further information about this subject. This might sound the same as the previous point, but here you're not ignoring other's help; you're incapable of recognizing that you're missing information to perform your task.

This affects you, and it affects the way your team deals with you. How can you work with someone who's incapable of accepting that they've made a mistake, or that they're not doing their best work?

Don't get me wrong; there is a big difference between confidence and ego. You can be completely confident about what you know you can do, and if your ego is in check you can know the extent of those capabilities. In contrast, an egocentric developer will cause a weird team dynamic, and other developers will try to avoid working with them. Honestly, why wouldn't they? Remember, you'll always be learning, so anytime you think you've finished learning everything about a topic, think again. Be open to being corrected, and every time you are, double-check the facts before disregarding the suggestion as incorrect.

The ideal developer's mindset, if you ask me, is that of an eternal student, always learning and always humble enough to recognize they can't know it all, ever.

YOU THINK YOU CAN DO EVERYTHING

Being self-sufficient is not necessarily a good quality in software development. Or rather, let me rephrase that: just because you *can* do everything doesn't mean you *should*. Being self-sufficient is good if that translates into you being flexible, capable of taking on different tasks throughout the duration of your project. However, that is miles away from trying to do everything yourself.

As developers, sometimes we fall under the illusion that because we can code, we can code everything, and there is no need to depend on anyone else, not even on third-party libraries. That's a dangerous route to travel, since in theory it's true. You could take the time needed to code a zero-dependencies project. However, in practice, it can become a time sink, increasing the timeline of your project exponentially, and even worse, your code will become a liability. Let me explain why that is:

- *You're wasting everyone's time.* Yes, you can code every piece of software related to your project, but take a second to look past your own ego. What is everyone else doing? Do their tasks depend on the completion of yours? What about the project's deadlines? Are they still in line with the time it'll take you to finish everything you suddenly seem to have to do? These are all questions that you always need to ask yourself, unless, of course, you're looking for your teammates to hate you and your descendants for the next three generations.

- *You're not contributing to the stability of your project.* Consider how long you're planning on taking to complete these extra dependencies you want to build. Then add the time it'll take you to make sure everything you build is stable enough for production. How can you be sure that what you create and the tests you make are as good as the testing and hardening that the third-party libraries you're replacing went through? Those libraries have been public potentially for years, and users have tested them in unforeseen and uncommon scenarios. It's really hard to top that level of stability, and thinking you can do it all on your own is nothing short of foolish.

You may have the skills to work on every single piece of your project (congrats, you're great!), but that doesn't entitle you to do so. You're part of a team for two reasons, one of them being that tasks need to be parallelized as much as possible to decrease time to market. The other is that you can't be great at everything. You may be good enough, but that doesn't make you great; there is a reason why people tend to focus on particular technologies or skills. Testers will be much better than you at finding problems with your own creations, designers will be fantastic at putting a visual representation to your application, and frontend developers will be much better at writing efficient visual transitions and effects. The experience that they have and that you don't makes the difference. Don't ever forget that.

YOU THINK YOU KNOW MORE THAN OTHERS, AND IT'S YOUR JOB TO CORRECT THEM

Probably the ultimate form of ego we're always fighting against is the idea that not only are we better than others, but that it's our job to correct them. I'm speaking from experience—I've had to deal with developers like that, both as teammates and as a manager myself. They are very hard to work with because you either work the way they want to or they won't let you work. They might even go so far as to raise issues around the quality of your work until you comply with their ideals.

There is always a chance that some of their corrections are valid, and you should take them into consideration. However, they take it to the next level by turning every suggestion into an important one. The problem with this is that they're giving you the solution already completed; you didn't get to it on your own, so the associated learning that comes from the lesson is missed. Your problem is solved, but the next time you face it (or a similar one), you won't know how resolve it yourself.

As a rule of thumb, you should pursue the eternal student mindset (something we already covered in this chapter), so give these suggestions the benefit of the doubt and try them out *yourself.* However, if instead you're the one insisting others take your suggestions, consider that you're not really helping them. In fact, you're hindering their progress. We've already covered how making mistakes is something every developer needs to do—they will learn a lot from them—but if you keep calling them out and solving their problems before they even see them, they'll never outgrow you.

Mind you, I'm not suggesting you just turn your head whenever you see someone about to make a mistake. But consider the following:

- *Be respectful when pointing out a mistake.* Just because it's obvious to you doesn't make it obvious to the other person. Getting exasperated and angry at others because of what you consider to be an obvious mistake is not going to help them. Instead, it'll reduce their interest in getting help from you in the future.
- *Let them work it out for themselves.* If you want to, point out the problem (respectfully, of course), and leave them to solve it. Offer your help, and let them decide whether or not to take it. Let them come to you, if they choose to.

If you actually want to be helpful to your teammates, be open and mindful of their different skill levels; don't expect them to know everything you do. Your ego could be the downfall of your career, so be mindful of it and learn to keep it under control. The sooner you do so, the faster you'll grow.

7.2.3 *Learn how to work remotely*

In this day and age, the tendency is to allow for some kind of remote work in all programming roles. This can range from one or two days a week to companies that work fully distributed. And even if you go to the office every day of the week, chances are you'll still be working with colleagues in other locations. Given the current speed of the internet in most countries, it makes little sense for companies to limit themselves to local talent when they could be employing people from the entire world market.

Working remotely could make a lot of sense for you as well, because it will enable you to work for companies that are either far away in your country or even on another continent. Working remotely will also save you a lot of time that you would otherwise spend traveling to and from the office, even if it's only a local commute. That is quality of life right there, and if on top of that you manage to organize your working hours, you can also be involved in your family's daily routine or meet with friends while still doing your full eight hours daily. As I mentioned in chapter 6, a few years ago I worked remotely from home, and I was able to take my kids to school every day and pick them up with my wife. That was only possible thanks to me being able to save a full hour's commute from my home to the office every morning. Otherwise, I would have missed all those little moments with them.

Being able to work remotely can be a great plus for you and your employer. However, it's not as simple as having an internet connection. I've met many developers who simply could not work remotely, not because they didn't like it but because they weren't capable of focusing enough on their work. They would get distracted by things like the TV, people passing by, or just their regular house chores. In fact, there are studies that have found that, indeed, factors such as children passing by, distractions such as the TV, the lack of human contact with colleagues, or simply a lack of physical activity from not having to get out of the house can cause both physical and mental health issues.[1] So keep the following in mind when applying for a fully or partially remote position:

- *Even if you're not physically present, you need to be available.* This is especially true if you're working on a remote team that relies on synchronous communication. If you all share a time zone (or close enough, anyway), the chances are you're likely to be expected to reply if you receive a chat message. That would be the equivalent of a colleague nudging your shoulder in the office. If, on the other hand, you're working with people from all over the world, your team is likely to rely on asynchronous communication (such as emails and persistent chat messages). In this scenario, I wouldn't say you're expected to reply immediately, but you are expected to reply when you're supposed to be working. This means you can't really decide unilaterally when and for how long you're going to be working simply because you're "working on your own," because you're not. Not feeling that you're still part of a team while working remotely is a big red flag that you need to be aware of.

- *Being available doesn't mean 24/7.* This is the B side to the previous point: you need to understand when you're *not* working, and avoid replying during that

---

[1] Yijing Xiao, Burcin Becerik-Gerber, Gale Lucas, and Shawn C. Roll, "Impacts of Working From Home During COVID-19 Pandemic on Physical and Mental Well-Being of Office Workstation Users," *J Occup Environ Med.* 63, no. 3 (March 2021): 181–190, www.ncbi.nlm.nih.gov/pmc/articles/PMC7934324.

time. Keeping a healthy life/work balance when working remotely is not easy, and the temptation to answer quick emails or to send information with just two taps on your mobile phone is always there. But if you go down that rabbit hole, there is no coming back. By the time you realize you're always working, you're so deep in the hole that there is no coming out again. Don't overwork (at least not for free).

- *Respect everyone's time.* This is crucial for all teams, and it shows that you acknowledge everyone else and respect them. For remote teams, this is even more relevant, considering that not everyone might share your time zone. For meetings, communications, and any other type of interaction you may have, consider the other person's schedule. If you're sending an invite to meet with someone, check their public calendar if you have access to it, or ask for several available slots for you to pick from. If you're sending them a direct message, consider their working hours; sometimes other developers might be drawn into working extra hours due to this practice. Their time is just as valuable as yours is, and if you'd hate it if you had to answer chat messages at 9 p.m., they probably do too.

- *Learn to draw the line between the office and your life.* As I've already mentioned, just because you're working from home (or remotely in a nearby location), it doesn't mean your work and life need to be the same. You'll need a way to unplug from your work and connect to your personal routine. This can be as simple as closing the laptop, going for a walk, or stepping away from the home office (if you have one) and relaxing on the couch. However you unplug, your mind needs to relax and disconnect. Working remotely does not equate to working more than you're paid for, so don't blur that line and don't let anyone blur it for you, either. If you get a message outside your normal working hours, it's perfectly fine to ignore it, even if you're just sitting in front of the TV not watching anything. You have every right to do so—it's your personal time, after all.

- *Respect your company's security policies.* Working from the office used to make this a lot simpler. The company network would have everything unwanted or untrusted blocked, and your workstation would be directly updated whenever required. Under a remote regime, however, you can get away with a lot more than when you're using a company workstation, since you're working from within your own house using your regular internet connection. However, companies do try to establish security policies that you should learn and follow, such as keeping your OS updated, or resetting your password after a certain number of days. Sometimes those requirements can be annoying, but it's a lot easier to follow them than to have your workstation blocked and need to be sent physically to IT because you didn't comply with your employer's security policies.

A successful remote working environment requires the company to instill a remote-first approach. However, you also need to do your part, and the preceding tips will give you a good start.

7.2.4   *Be social*

Developers aren't social animals; they're lonely nerds who sit in front of a computer 20 hours a day, aren't they? That, of course, is not true. One of the keys to a successful working environment and a performant and tight team is socialization.

Yes, there are days I wish I could just open my laptop at 8 a.m. and close it later at 6 p.m. without having said a word to a single individual. However, that's not only not possible, but it's the worst thing I could do for myself. We're developers, but we're also people, and by nature we're social animals. That doesn't mean you have to go out and party or talk to strangers in clubs, unless you enjoy that. All I'm saying is that you should acknowledge that your team is composed of other people with their own interests, their own problems, and their own aspirations, just like you. If you don't make the effort to get to know them, you'll never truly be part of that team.

On your first day at a new job, assuming you're all colocated, it's normal tradition to invite the new member out to lunch. No, they're not going to pay for your meal, but at least you'll eat with the group and get to know their names and personalities. If that happens, make the effort to go through with it. Sharing a meal can help you connect with them more quickly. Let them get to know you and answer questions with details—don't just stick to the classics of "no" and "yes."

If, on the other hand, you're joining a remote team, getting to know people can be more difficult, but these are some tricks that can help you connect with others faster:

- *Enable your camera on all meetings.* If you don't like having the camera on, make sure you do it for the first few days to give everyone a chance to see your face and your reactions. Then update your avatar with an updated picture and disable the cam.
- *Be active in your team calls.* This is especially important if you don't have a camera or you don't want to enable it. If you're quiet in a virtual meeting, you're not there. It's that simple. Speak up and let others know you're there. Just make sure you have something meaningful to add to the conversation. On remote-first teams, you'll likely have some sessions with the team so that you can get to know each other. Speak up, and don't be afraid to show a bit of yourself—give details, share your hobbies, and so on. You never know what will click with others.
- *Join the social virtual meetings.* I know, you probably hate meetings. But if you're working remotely, the only chance you have to socialize with your teammates is through these types of virtual calls. Enable the camera, get a cup of coffee, tea, or whatever you like to drink, and join the conversation. You may not participate a lot at first, but these meetings will probably be hosted by HR people looking to integrate new joiners into the company culture and into their own teams. Chances are you'll get some help from them as well. Don't be shy, join!
- *If you have chat channels for sharing personal information or even jokes, participate on them.* Maybe you don't have anything to share there, but at least you'll interact with others. A "that's funny" here and a "LOL" there can go a long way. Trust me, these random channels help a lot to alleviate the stress of the daily routine, and they help you see who's the clown of the team.

Socializing is not strictly part of your tasks, but it will definitely help you integrate into a team as a new joiner. Not only that, but by taking you out of your working mindset, it will also help you release stress, diminish burnout, and battle the feeling of loneliness (even if you're just socializing remotely). The simple reason why it's so good for our mental health is because it's the natural thing to do! We're social animals, whether you like it or not, and your mind and body are asking for it. So my recommendation is that you consider it to be one of your tasks. Don't ignore it, thinking that you have more important things to do. *This is important.*

7.3 Working on your own skills

Let's focus a bit on you, shall we? Getting the manager to love you is crucial, as is fitting in with your team. But you need to care for your own self-improvement from time to time. After all, learning doesn't just happen (although sometimes I wish it did, trust me).

Imagine, if you will, that you've been working at this new job for about a month and a half, and you're starting to get it. You've gone through the onboarding process, you've learned the custom framework they're using, and now you're starting to close tasks on your own. You're finally doing it—you're a somewhat autonomous developer. Yay!

But there's still something missing. You can't really put your finger on it, but you have this feeling of not being good enough, not yet. You can feel the eyes of your manager piercing you, looking for a sign that you're special, and then looking away disappointed. Your teammates talk about new technologies and new frameworks they can't wait to try, but they never include you in those conversations, as if they know something you don't. Are you going to be fired? Are they going to finally realize you passed the interview by mistake and you have no idea what you're doing more often than not? What is happening!?

I'm willing to bet that 99% of the time, nothing is wrong. That's just your impostor syndrome kicking in. Congrats, you passed the final test, you're a developer now! The impostor syndrome is a psychological pattern in which the person doubts their skills, knowledge, and accomplishments. They constantly feel like they're about to be discovered as a fraud in front of everyone.

Does that sound familiar? It's okay if it does—according to a study from Blind, almost 58% of all developers working for FAANG (Facebook, Amazon, Apple, Netflix, and Google) feel that way.[2] And don't feel special just yet—according to research by Jaruwan Sakulku and James Alexander, almost 70% of people from different personal and professional backgrounds feel it.[3]

Why am I talking about this, and what can you do to solve it? The first thing to understand is that I'm not a psychologist, and my advice only comes from personal

---

[2] "58 Percent of Tech Workers Feel Like Impostors," *Blind* blog (Sept. 5, 2018), https://www.teamblind .com/blog/index.php/2018/09/05/58-percent-of-tech-workers-feel-like-impostors/.

[3] Jaruwan Sakulku and James Alexander, "The Impostor Phenomenon," *International Journal of Behavioral Science*, 6, no. 1 (2011): 73-92, https://www.sciencetheearth.com/uploads/2/4/6/5/24658156/2011_sakulku_the _impostor_phenomenon.pdf.

experience, having felt this way often in the past and still feeling it today from time to time. This is a very real thing that happens in our industry, and it is fostered by the way our industry works. We sometimes worship developers who create tools and libraries that millions of other developers use. We hope that one day we'll be as good as they are, but we forget that we already are. We see a lot of online "celebrities" within our industry, with tens or even hundreds of thousands of followers pushing content every day, and we feel tiny compared to them. But we're not, and we need to remember that.

Overcoming, or at least learning to cope with, impostor syndrome is not easy, but it centers around understanding that you have what it takes to make it. Boost your self confidence to a point where you feel comfortable enough with your peers. How can you do that? One path I recommend is improving your own skills. Working on them will show others and (more importantly) yourself that you're doing something to improve, to better yourself.

7.3.1   Continuous learning

Step one is to keep learning. We all know this by now—your software development career stops progressing the moment you stop learning. So let's not stop, shall we?

You'll find learning opportunities popping up all the time, so try not to ignore them all. Pick one every now and then, and follow through. Which one should you pick? That's really up to you. But since we're discussing team-related topics here, I recommend considering your current context when making that decision. Are you struggling with the current framework of your project? Or perhaps the language itself feels a bit alien to you? Improving those skills will not only benefit you, but your team as well. That's what I call a win-win.

Depending on the company you work for, one of several things can happen:

- *They might provide the learning experience themselves.* The company may provide internal training or perhaps grant their employees direct access to learning portals such as Udemy or Pluralsight. This is good, because on the one hand, they are showing that they care about the education level of their employees, and they want you to keep growing. On the other hand, it's also great because by signing up for these training sessions, you're directly showing them that you care about the same thing. They'll be keeping an eye on what you're doing and how it goes.

- *They might provide a training budget you can take advantage of.* Some companies have a training budget that can be used by employees. You may have to go out and find the course you want to take and figure out how much it's going to cost, but your company will either pay the full price or help out with a percentage.

- *They may not have any way to help you.* Not every company is capable of financially helping you or even interested in doing so. This makes things a bit harder, but it's still not impossible, considering how many learning resources are online these days.

Whatever your employer's policy is toward your continuous training, it's always going to be up to you. Don't get discouraged if you're working for a company that just says "Sorry, but we have no way to help you there." You can do it without them—not a problem.

So what can you do? Where can you improve your skills, and why should you pay money instead of getting it for free? All great questions! The first thing you need to do is pick the topic you want to improve on. As I already mentioned, it's completely up to you, but if you're expecting your teammates and employer to appreciate the effort you're making, it should be something related to their needs. Mind you, I think there is a huge benefit to learning about technologies that are very far from what you do daily, like doing a Unity course (Unity being one of the biggest game-development platforms around) on creating 2D platformers, if you work with microcontrollers daily. That's probably not going to be seen as directly beneficial by your team, but it will broaden your horizons and show you something that you would have never learned otherwise. That's also a way to indirectly improve your skills, so don't limit yourself.

Once you've decided what you want to improve on, the next step is to pick a learning platform. There are many out there that are very good, such as these:

- *Udemy (www.udemy.com)*—Udemy has varied courses with multiple levels of difficulty. They also often have a $10 course promotion that allows you to pick up expensive training for a fraction of the cost.
- *Pluralsight (www.pluralsight.com)*—While you can take single courses, like with Udemy and others, Pluralsight offers preset learning paths that you can follow to make the most out of your effort. This is the perfect way to go from zero to expert without having to decide what to learn next.
- *Educative (www.educative.io)*—If learning through video is not your thing, Educative offers written courses on many different programming topics. They have interactive sections in which you can practice what you learn.
- *Coursera (www.coursera.org)*—If you're looking for more academic-oriented courses, either because of the topics you want to learn about or because you learn better that way, Coursera is for you. They have partnered with over 200 universities and offer, in some cases, full degrees through their online platform.

This list can be as long as you want, because there are many more learning platforms. Don't get caught up with the number of choices. If you're starting out, pick one of the most common providers and go with it. If you don't like the experience, you can switch and try a new one. However, these are the most common platforms with the highest-rated options.

If, on the other hand, you're looking to train yourself without spending any money, there are alternatives. If you like learning through videos, searching for the topics you're interested in on YouTube is your best bet. Otherwise, you'll be better off searching Google for tutorials and articles related to your interests. A common place to find these tutorials is Medium.com, which concentrates a lot of programming knowledge through multiple publications about our industry (they're like mini blogs inside Medium). If you pay for the Medium membership of $5 a month (I know we we're talking about not paying a dime, but hear me out), you get access to the entire catalog of Pragmatic Programming books (https://medium.com/@pragprog). That's a lot of books and knowledge for just $5 a month.

One could argue that given the amount of free access that you can get by Googling for tutorials, it makes no sense to pay for online courses. But the truth is, you can't really certify that you've learned a topic well enough on your own, whereas the preceding learning platforms will give you some kind of completion certificate that you can share with your employers and teammates if so required. Beyond that, you may also need the guidance a learning platform offers, or the potential interaction with other students. Whatever the case, learning through online, paid platforms is an option that you should not dismiss simply because there are free alternatives.

7.3.2 *Measuring your learning progress*

Once you start learning, the next thing you'll naturally want to know is how you are progressing on your path to becoming proficient in the topic you've picked. The classic mistake we make in this situation is to compare our progress with that of others going through a similar process, and especially with those who actively share it online. That is the worst thing you can do.

Whether you're comparing yourself with a colleague or with someone you follow on Twitter, what you'll see is what they let you see, which is usually the results and not the process. You can see that they've mastered a new skill or perhaps understood a new concept, and you'll immediately compare it with your own progress and get depressed if you're not there yet. The problem with that is that you're not making a fair comparison. When you look at yourself, you see all the struggles you're going through, all the problems you've found along the way, and all the times you thought about giving up. But when you look at the other person, you only see the results and assume they had no issues. In reality, they could have struggled more than you. If you're looking for a perfect recipe to trigger that impostor syndrome I talked about, this is it.

How can you know if you're actually making progress? Don't look at anyone else but you. Compare your current state with your own state from the past. That's the only true metric you should care about.

If you're following a preset path like one you'd get from Pluralsight or Coursera, your progress will be determined by how far along you are. However, if you're learning from random tutorials and videos, set some goals before you start. Decide where you want to get to, and then start planning backward toward your current state. For example, if you're looking to build a 2D platformer, but you've always worked in web development, what would be your learning path? Where would you start learning? Your end goal is to create a 2D platformer, so set that at the end of your timeline and do some research. What goes into creating a game like that? Your character needs to move around and interact with the world and the enemies, so there is a physical component.

Make a note: "2D physics for game development." But before getting there, you need to have something to move around, so write down "Add 2D character to game." How do you control your character? Write down "2D character control." Your character also has to move around somewhere, so it's time for "2D level design and implementation." That would require you to know how to structure your game code and load a level, so perhaps write down "Game loop and internal architecture."

Alright, let's trace our path:

1 Game loop and internal architecture
2 2D level design and implementation
3 2D character control
4 Add 2D character to game
5 2D physics for game development

Perhaps now you have the basics for a game—at least the minimum viable product (MVP) version of it. You have the basic idea of what you want to do—the main game mechanics. The rest is just figuring out what you're missing and doing the same exercise. For example, you're probably missing music and sound effects. Try to reverse your path into that one.

Finally, if you need to, set yourself a time limit. That will be another way you can motivate yourself. Knowing that you need to complete this curriculum in under two months, for example, will make sure you don't slack off or procrastinate too much. You can track your progress inside your own timeline and measure how much you've learned based on your own experiments and insights.

Just make sure that when you create this learning curriculum and set a timeline for it, you don't shoot yourself in the foot. You know more than anyone else how much time you have to spend on this and how badly you need it. Use that knowledge to set a reasonable timetable.

7.3.3 *Learning from code reviews*

Finally, another way of learning that does not involve money being spent or extra time away from work is to learn from your colleagues. Code reviews are a perfect way to capture that knowledge, especially if they're done right.

Code reviews are sessions in which colleagues review your code before it's marked as "ready for production," to make sure you haven't introduced bad practices or unwanted bugs. Sadly, not everyone understands that. Learning to take criticism is a skill we have to develop. It's a great source of knowledge, after all—we just need to learn how to tap it.

The main thing to understand about code reviews is that they're not personal. If you don't understand this, you won't get any of the benefits. During the review session, you'll normally be asked to explain the code you've worked on. You'll explain the problem you were trying to solve, the logic behind your solution, and any particular technical choices you made. Normally this takes place as a conversation between you and your reviewers. They'll listen to you for a while, and then they'll start asking questions, mainly the dreaded "Why?" but don't worry. If you wrote that code, you'll know why you did what you did, so you'll be able to answer those questions.

You can receive feedback like the following:

- *Typos or grammar errors in your comments*—Yes, some teams review even the comments you write, and if you think about it, it makes sense. The comments are just as important as the code you wrote, if you're expecting anyone else to understand your code and maintain it in the future. Writing comments with proper grammar is important.

- *Logical mistakes in your solution*—This is the classic problem: when you start explaining how you solved the problem, they might point out that you forgot some edge cases, or you went about solving the problem in the wrong way. This doesn't necessarily involve your code, but the logic around it. It's important that if you get this type of feedback, you also ask as many questions as you can until you fully understand where the error lies and how you can solve it. Either that, or schedule a follow-up meeting to discuss the topic if your reviewers don't have the time to do it at the time.

- *Incorrect or missing coding standards*—This is another easy one to spot. If your reviewers have been coding in your team longer than you, they'll have these rules more internalized than you, and they'll be better able to identify when you've missed them. These are easy to fix—they usually involve naming standards, removing magic numbers into constants somewhere else, and the like. A good idea here is to take notes of all these mini issues and tackle them together as part of the same fix.

- *Bugs*—This is probably the worst thing that can be found in your code: problems added by the way you coded the solution. This can happen to anyone, and it's not necessarily a bad thing, but it's something you need to own and fix once the review is over. If a bug is found during the review of your code, make sure you fully understand what the bug implies and what you have to do to remove it. Just like with logical mistakes, if discussing the solution will take too long, consider setting up a follow-up meeting to discuss it further.

A successful code review is one you come out of having learned something new about your code, the solution, or the way your team works. To do that, make sure you ask about every little detail related to the feedback you receive, and don't be afraid to say "I don't understand" if the explanations aren't clear enough. Not every developer knows how to explain complex topics well, and sometimes something that is obvious to your reviewer might not be obvious to you. That is perfectly fine.

Summary

- Getting your manager's attention and interest is crucial for your professional progress. You can do so by providing updates about your status, often using the preestablished task-tracking system, understanding how to behave in meetings, properly planning your work, and avoiding reinventing the wheel when applicable.

- Learn to get along with the testing team. They're not there to highlight your mistakes, but rather to ensure that you all build a stable product.

- Don't let your ego get the best of you. All developers have that problem at the start of their career, but only great developers learn how to control it and keep it from hindering their progress and the way they relate to their teams. Consider the way you interact with your teammates, and adjust it if you recognize some of the behaviors I mentioned in this chapter.

- Understand that working remotely does not just mean working from home. It also means being there on time, showing up when you're needed, taking into account your teammates' time zones and, most importantly, taking care of your work/life balance. Remote work provides a lot of benefits for developers by giving them flexibility in their working schedule and saving potentially hours of commutes. However, you need to commit to following the standards set by the company around this practice.

- Socializing with your team is just as important as doing good work and writing quality code. Whether you're physically going to the office or interacting with everyone remotely, you, as the new team member joining the team, need to make an effort to make sure others get to know you.

- Remember that impostor syndrome is real and quite common in our industry. There are multiple things you can do to combat it, one of them being working on improving your own skills.

- Make sure you keep learning new things and compare your progress with yourself. Everyone learns at different rates and through different processes, so comparing your progress with that of others is only going to give you an unrealistic view of your progress.

Understanding
team leadership

8

This chapter covers

- What makes a great leader
- Hard truths to hear from your leader
- Why most software projects take longer than expected
- How to properly correct your team lead
- How to speak properly to a client
- The importance of feedback, and best practices around it

You're not a leader yet, or you would probably not be reading this book. Why, then, are we talking about team leaders in the final chapter of the book?

This chapter is not meant to teach you how to be a leader—that will come with time and experience. Right now, I'm looking to give you a glimpse into what your leader is going through, to give you some understanding of why they do what they do, and also to show you what you can expect once you reach a leadership position.

If you're going to get only one thing out of this chapter, make sure it's the understanding of what a leader has to deal with on any given project. You can use that to connect with them on your own project.

8.1 Understanding your leader

The first thing we'll do is take a deep dive into your leader's inner workings. There is a reason why they do what they do, so it's useful to understand how leaders think and work.

We sometimes tend to think leaders are like firefighters, going from one fire to the next, solving problems reactively and without having a day's rest to plan. That's not the right leadership ideal, nor is it the right way to think of a leader. Yes, they do have to deal with problems all the time, but the signature characteristic of a great leader is that they also have an eye set on the future. They're always thinking about the end goal. This ability to tackle the problems of today and also plan for the problems of tomorrow is what makes a leader so necessary.

8.1.1 Key traits of a good leader

You'll be hard pressed to find all of the following traits in a single person—that would make them a near-perfect leader. However, you can use the following list to measure how close to perfection they get:

- *They like to challenge the status quo*. Leaders don't like to follow rules or do what everyone else is doing simply because it fits the status quo. They have enough confidence in their skills to decide for themselves what the best course of action is, and they don't let outside influences direct their decisions. Of course, no leader works alone, apart from the rest of the world; outside influences can and should affect the decisions taken, but only when the leader considers it appropriate. A good leader should foster feedback loops to validate their ideas, both within their team and in the industry they're working for. A great leader will not only push for innovation themselves but will also foster that challenging mindset in their own teams.

- *They set clear expectations for everything*. Managing expectations is a mantra for leaders the same way "location, location, location" is for real estate agents. It's key to everything they do. By managing the expectations of the stakeholders they interact with, managers can maintain a healthy relationship with their clients and foster trust in their team's skills. Properly setting the team's expectations regarding their tasks and responsibilities also helps everyone understand what they need to work on and what the priorities are. If you, as a team member, don't know exactly what your leader is expecting of you, you'll have to make assumptions regarding the extent of your responsibilities, and assumptions can lead to mistakes and misunderstandings. Expectations can range across the list of tasks to work on, their delivery dates, the depth of the analysis required, and so on. The point is to make sure that whoever the leader is interacting with knows exactly what to expect from that exchange.

- *They create a clear plan for success.* Whatever they're working on, the leader needs the endeavor to succeed, which is why they're always planning. That plan involves everyone on the team, and the leader usually assigns a role for each person to follow. Your assigned roles are a reflection of what the leader sees in you based on the interactions you've had with them. If you're not happy with the role you're assigned in your project or with the type of tasks you're assigned, speak up. A great leader will understand that the plan needs to be agreed on by everyone and that others might have suggestions that would make the plan better.

- *They prioritize the team over themselves.* The project needs to succeed, and that will only happen if the team is happy, able to work, and motivated to do so. When it comes to actually developing a feature or testing a new release, leaders have very little to say or do. They don't matter at that stage. A great leader understands this and their place in the team. Above everything else, the team needs to be happy, or nothing else will work. A great leader is one who accepts responsibility for the failures of the project instead of blaming their team, and one who is happy about the team's successes when things work out for the best.

- *They're constantly looking for sustainable results.* Just as you are not alone, even if you're the only developer in your team, leaders aren't working in a vacuum either. They need to show that the success of their team and their project can be sustained over time, repeated in the following iterations, and duplicated in subsequent projects. This is why they're sometimes a bit obsessed with results and metrics. While you might want to focus on reaching 80% code coverage on your tests, they'll be more interested in looking at burndown charts showing the decreased pending work for the overall plan This means they'll need you to give them updates and to update the task-tracking software often (which we covered in chapter 7).

- *They're constantly trying to improve themselves.* Reaching a leadership position is not the end of the journey. It's actually the beginning of a new one, which means that when someone reaches that point, there are a lot of skills they have to learn. On top of that, IT leaders also have to keep updating themselves about the technologies related to their industry, because those also keep evolving. If they only focus on their leadership skills, they'll quickly be outdated technology-wise. Great IT leads have the double challenge of constantly improving their leadership skills and their tech skills to keep up with the industry and their clients.

- *They build networks and are always looking for external collaboration.* Leaders understand that they're not doing the hard work of pushing the code and the features forward. They're also humble enough to understand that sometimes the talent they need might not be inside their own team. For whatever reason, that talent might be part of another team or, in some cases, in other organizations. A great leader will always try to get the best results, and if they have to reach outside of their immediate circle of influence and contact others, they'll move heaven and earth to do so. It's not about ego with leaders, but instead about results. Keep that in mind when they suggest you collaborate with someone else. It's not a reflection of your inability to do something, but rather a potential learning experience waiting to happen.

Can you identify any of these characteristics in your current leader or perhaps in yourself? If so, that's good! That means you (or your leader) are doing something right! On the other hand, if you can't find an overlap between the preceding list and the way your leader works, you might want to start either looking for a new lead (which may mean requesting a change of project or changing companies), or perhaps showing them how to be a better leader by incorporating some of these behaviors into your own daily work.

One major point from the list is the one about setting the right expectations, especially when things aren't working out. For a leader, having a conversation with someone who's not performing or who's not adding the value they should be adding to the team is hard. The key to that conversation relies on, you guessed it, setting the right expectations.

8.1.2　Hard truths to hear from your leader

Your leader is not out to get you—that's the first thing you have to understand when having a tough conversation with them. The conversation is not about them and it's definitely not about you. Instead, it's about the message they're trying to convey, and they're most likely saying it because you need to hear it.

Hearing negative words coming from your manager is not easy, but you have to remember that you're hearing them because your manager is giving you the opportunity to change the situation. Unless the words are "You're fired," you can treat this as a learning opportunity. Let's take a quick look at four criticisms your manager might make.

YOU CAN'T DO THAT

Imagine the following scenario: you, after two weeks working on the same task, finally realize your code can be developed a bit more and turned into an independent library that can be reused by others in your company. "This is a great idea," you think, and rightfully so.

You proceed to run to your manager's desk and tell them about it. With possibly one more week, or two at most, you can have this new library ready. Then, with a bit of work refactoring the dependent code, you can add it as a dependency to the current project. You're thinking about the future of the company here, and you weren't asked to do so, which means you're being proactive. There is no way this can't be a good thing.

But your manager looks at you and simply says "You can't do that, not right now ..." You don't even hear the rest of the sentence. You feel numb, and the excitement you had running through your body is slowly going away, leaving you exhausted. You have to go back to your boring task now. End of scene.

Does that feel familiar? What do you think was in the rest of your manager's sentence that you didn't hear?

I've been through that experience many times, as a developer and as a manager. It's very common, but it's important to understand one thing: it's not personal. This is not necessarily negative feedback, but it can feel that way if you're not used to hearing it. If you've been working on your own for a while, you've never had a leader telling you "no." Once you become part of a team, you're not the center of everything, and your priorities and preferences aren't the only thing that count anymore. Your leader will undoubtedly have to take everybody's needs and preferences into consideration, not to mention the project's timeline.

That means the "no" you're getting from your leader isn't because they don't like you, and it's not because they think your idea is silly or dumb. It's a "no" because from a resource-utilization point of view, it makes no sense. You're not obligated to know that beforehand, so don't feel bad about that either.

Usually the only person with a bird's-eye view of the project is the leader. They're constantly looking at the big picture because that's their job, while yours is normally to focus on one particular task or feature. Don't get me wrong, though. The level of detail you know about your task is considerably greater than your lead knows about it. You can't be expected to know about whether your idea fits within the current timeline, but you can still propose it.

Just because you're getting "no" as a response doesn't mean you should stop coming up with new suggestions. That's invaluable for a leader—you're proactively trying to improve the project, so don't stop. However, when you do get "no" as a response, try to understand why, so you can adapt your proposal next time.

YOU HAVE A PROBLEM

You probably do have a problem, and the best thing you can do is accept it. I've had to say this many times in the past. It's not an easy conversation to have, but if the situation reached this point, it means you've probably gone through some previous conversations where your manager tried to show that you were underperforming somehow.

The fact that you're having this conversation means you've not really paid attention to those previous discussions, and your performance has been affected. In other words, the conversation is necessary, and the worst thing you can do is deny the problem.

You should be critical of what you're being told, but try to be objective about it. If they're saying you have a problem, there is a good chance that you do, so don't waste time denying it or justifying your actions. That will not help anyone, and it will not retroactively solve your performance problems.

Instead, focus on solving the problem. Ask whatever you have to, as many times as you need to. If the feedback is not making sense, request a clarification—not to understand the problem, but with the aim of finding a solution and getting your performance back on track.

There is a caveat, though: leaders can be wrong. I know, it's a hard pill to swallow (especially for them), but it happens. They can be wrong about the feedback because they might have received it from someone else with an incomplete perception of your work. Or perhaps they've been evaluating you without really getting to know what you do and instead have only focused on what they've heard about you.

Imagine having spent your first three months in a new company working relentlessly on your tasks, delivering everything on time, but having barely any contact with your manager. Maybe you've been put under the tutelage of a more senior member, and that person is directly managing you. When it's time to evaluate you, your actual manager only takes into consideration the work he's seen from you, which in this context is none. Maybe the senior member has been absorbing the responsibility for everything you've done. This manager would have the wrong idea about your work, and they would probably think you're not really adding the value you were meant to be adding.

In such situations, you still need to be objective, but as a result of that mindset, you should also be able to speak up and state your case. Do not provide a knee-jerk response, and do not get offended or be disrespectful, but make sure you clearly show the work you've done and that you'd like a reevaluation based on your actual performance.

Whoever is evaluating you has the power to affect your career in both positive and negative ways, which means they should have all the information before making such an important decision.

YOUR PLAN IS WRONG

You'll be hearing this one often, especially if you're trying to propose changes or new developments during the first stages of your career. Suggesting changes requires a lot more than focusing on the code aspects of the project.

Don't get me wrong, any developer making suggestions and proposing improvements is a developer who worries about the well being of the project, someone who's always looking to improve and do more interesting work. That's valuable, and you should not stop it, even if you keep getting pushback from above. However, you do have to understand that when you're trying to propose something to your manager, they will look at it in this order:

1 They'll try to understand what problem you're trying to solve.
2 They'll skim over the technical proposal to identify any potential issues.
3 They'll quickly look for the section of your proposal that covers the type of team required and the timeline for it.
4 If the previous steps make sense, they'll go back to the tech proposal and review it properly.

Why will they do this? Because they need to understand the impact of your proposal on the already established plan. Remember that bird's-eye view I mentioned before? That's what they care about most.

Take that into account when making your next proposal. The actual implementation of whatever you want to change is important, but your focus needs to be on the plan and the time you're estimating it'll take to implement. If you don't provide that information, the proposal will be rejected.

"YOU HAVE TO LEARN X"

Ugh, you're telling me that after all the courses and tutorials I went through to understand *Y*, I now need to pick up *X*? I quit!

Yeah, you'll be hearing that you need to learn new skills often, especially when you're getting started in your journey, and that's fine. In fact, it's not only fine, it's perfect, because there is so much to learn that you might suffer from what some people call "analysis paralysis." You'll start looking at all the potential learning avenues, and you may freeze, unable to make a decision. If your manager or leader is telling you exactly what you need to pick up, they're giving you the answer to that question. That's perfect!

The key here is not to let this take you down. You may think that you should have seen the request coming, or you should have been more proactive, and perhaps you should have learned this on your own before anybody told you about it. Perhaps that's true. But getting that kind of awareness and precognition, if you will, takes years. You have to know the team, know the company, understand the ecosystem, and be aware of where it's going before you can predict what you should learn next.

With that in mind, don't take the fact that your manager is telling you what to learn as a bad thing. They could have said, "You're fired because you haven't learned *X* yet." Instead, they're giving you a chance to improve and catch up to where they need you to be, so take it.

8.1.3 *Constantly asking for status updates*

Ah, the good old "Hey <insert your name here>, how's that task going? Are you going to finish it on time?" I know what you're thinking: "Well <insert your leader's name here>, if you'd stop asking me about it every 10 minutes, I would!" But don't be so harsh on your leader. There is a reason why they keep asking: you're not doing your job.

Let me explain before you close the book and throw it out the window! The reason why leaders are constantly bugging you about the progress of your task is because they're managing a project, and a project has a timeline to fit into, a budget to be developed, and stakeholders who have a particular interest in seeing the project published and production ready. All of that means your leader is stuck between the proverbial rock and a hard place. The rock is all those stakeholders, timelines, budgets, and other external factors pressuring them. The hard place is you and the rest of the team pushing code and finishing tasks without properly updating the task-tracking software, or making changes without checking how they'll affect the timeline.

That's why they keep asking for an update—as a leader, they're responsible for how the team works and its results. If you only focus on your code, and you neglect giving them a daily status update, you render them effectively blind.

Part of being a good leader is knowing exactly what your team is working on and if they'll be on time or if there will be some kind of delay on the delivery of the current work iteration. But they can't do it on their own. Great leaders don't work in a vacuum—they are great because their teams are great, and that involves them providing timely warnings about delays or potential setbacks. Your job as a developer is not just to deliver code but also to keep your leader updated about potential problems or areas of improvement that you find. The more you communicate, the better.

Of course, you can't overdo it and overwhelm them with information. There are channels for this, and you should use them properly:

- If there is an urgent problem, like a build failure or a sudden blocker that's not letting you work anymore, a direct message is recommended.
- If you have an idea for an improvement over a current process, an email should be more than enough. You could potentially follow that email with a presentation.
- If you have questions or you've found something that will delay the delivery of one particular task, the ideal place to mention this and to have a discussion is on the task-tracking system. That way all the relevant information is displayed in the same place. Usually these apps allow you to add comments.

8.1.4 Understanding task assignments

Always having to do the same type of task can be a frustrating experience. When you're just getting started, you may be writing unit tests, but in other situations it might be something else. The point is usually not what you're doing, but that you're doing it over and over again. Why do you think they do that?

Great leaders worry about their teams and their professional growth. That's partially because the better a developer you are, the more value you add, but it's also because people who learn and grow are motivated to stay, especially when there is an internal push to keep that growth happening. One of the many things I've mentioned throughout this book is that we learn by doing and by making mistakes, and one way that leaders have to steer us in the right direction is through task assignments.

Sometimes they'll assign you tasks that you've never done before, so you can research and pick up a new skill. If the task is urgent and needs to be completed quickly, they'll likely assign it to someone who's familiar with that kind of work, but if that's not the case, they'll try to mix things up and keep it interesting. If you're getting the same type of task, such as unit tests, chances are they're trying to tell you that you still have a few more things to learn about them before moving on to something else. Perhaps you're taking too long, or perhaps you're not covering the right types of scenarios, or you're not using the right methodology to create them. If you don't know why you're repeatedly being assigned a particular task, the best thing you can do is have a direct conversation with your leader and ask.

Through that conversation, you might find out that your project is going through some problems, and you're being assigned these types of tasks because you're quite fast and good at them. Although you might hate them, you at least know why you're the one doing them. It's not because your manager hates you or doesn't appreciate your work, but rather because they recognize your skills and are taking advantage of them (in a good way) to solve the problem they're having.

Remember that in normal software projects, there are usually a lot of things happening outside the scope of the developers. Never assume the decisions and actions your leader takes are based on personal hatred toward you or any other team member. Instead, try to have an honest and open dialog with your leader, and offer to help in any way you can to solve any problem. This is the right attitude to have, and it will be welcomed and appreciated by your leader.

8.2   *The 90-10 rule*

Have you ever thoroughly closed a project on your own? I'm not asking you if you've coded everything you had to code. That's a given. I'm asking you if you did everything else needed to close a software project.

There is a "funny because it's true" type of rule in the industry that says, "The first 90% of the project is finished within 10% of the time, while the last 10% of the project requires 90% of the time." Read that again and let it sink in. If you've done all your coding and you've managed to close all your tasks, why do you think your leader isn't calling it a day already? What else is there to do?

There are many reasons why projects can take longer than expected or be hard to close, and while those reasons aren't necessarily related to you, the developer, it's important for you to understand the type of issues your leader has to deal with.

Let's take a look at some of the most common reasons for delays, so you know how to identify them and can raise your hand as a warning, in case your leader hasn't picked up on them yet:

- *The dreaded scope creep*—All projects start with a somewhat defined backlog of work—the list of items that need to be completed for the project to be deemed "done." This list is first created at a high level and then detailed as you go along (for agile methodologies), or it's thoroughly detailed before writing the first line of code (in more traditional, waterfall-like methodologies). The scope creep happens when new features or changes are added to the original backlog. If more work is added, for whatever reason, more time needs to be estimated for the completion of the project. If instead tasks are added but the original estimates are not revised, you'll reach the point in time you had originally estimated you'd be done, but you'll still have a lot more to do.

  Adding work in the middle of a project development cycle is not unheard of. In fact, many agile methodologies embrace that practice, but they also cover the effect of that new workload on overall estimates. So if you see this happening to your project, and no one is raising their hands to talk about the effect it'll have on the overall delivery date, you might want to ask about it. In the worst-case scenario, your leader has already considered it; in the best case, you're bringing up a huge point and everyone will thank you for it.

- *Leaving unknowns for last*—I've already discussed assumptions several times in this book, so by now you should know that they are great for making estimations, but they don't always reflect reality. If you have many assumptions at the start of your project, leaving them for the end is not a great idea. You might end up realizing that most of them were wrong and that you need to adjust your plan and perhaps even your product. Instead try to validate your assumptions as soon as possible, and correct any affected estimates sooner rather than later. As a responsible developer, if you notice that you're working on a feature that's based on assumptions, you might want to raise your hand and speak up. Let everyone know that while you are perfectly capable of working on the feature, there is a huge risk of needing to rework the feature once the assumption is verified.

- *Having people work on multiple projects at once*—This is not unheard of, believe it or not, especially in consulting companies. These companies will try to maximize the profit they get from a developer by committing them to multiple projects, sometimes even having them working at 100% in all of them, which makes no sense (how can you be working full time on more than one thing at the same time?). The problem with this is that these projects tend to be independent of each other, have different priorities and, in some cases, their managers don't even know about the existence of the other. This puts the developer in the middle, having to deal with potentially conflicting priorities and having to decide which one takes precedence over the other, and they may end up picking the less relevant project or the wrong task to focus on. This responsibility should not be on the developer. If you happen to find yourself in this situation, make sure there is someone out there—someone who is outside of these projects—that knows about you and is capable of helping you make the difficult calls between conflicting priorities. That person can be a mentor, a manager, or perhaps even a senior manager who can interact and lead the managers pulling you in different directions. Each company will have a different hierarchical structure, so make sure you understand who above you can help you resolve problems like these.

- *Reworking features due to poor planning*—This can be seen as a specialized version of the assumptions problem. When a project starts and its features aren't properly defined with the level of detail required, developers will tend to make assumptions on their own. And we all know what happens with assumptions. In this case, the problem is even worse, because these assumptions will probably go unnoticed by everyone (even the developer who made them). By the time you're finishing the project and closing the features, these unconscious assumptions will come and bite you, causing you to reevaluate your life choices along with the decisions you made back then. Do not make assumptions if you can avoid them, and if you do, document them somewhere, ideally on the task-tracking software you're using. That way, you are notifying your leader, so they can validate the assumptions in time. Additionally, you're leaving a paper trail about what these assumptions were, so that when the time comes and the feature doesn't work as expected, everyone knows about them.

Projects are like wild animals when they start. There is a lot of room for chaos and for everything to go wrong. It's the leader's job to control that chaos and funnel it in the right direction. They can't do it on their own, though. It's your job to keep that in mind and provide them with as much help as you can, in addition to writing the code you're asked to write.

But what happens if your leader is wrong? What if they're making a mistake? Can that happen?

8.3   *Correcting your leader*

Let's set the scene: you're in the middle of the planning meeting for your project's next big feature. They're talking about the importance of keeping the test coverage up around 85%, and someone asks about the three endpoints that deal with storing data on the database. How are they going to test that the data is properly saved with their unit tests?

Your leader quickly steps up and proposes a strategy that has a disposable database boot up inside a Docker container as part of the testing script. Because you've been reading this book, you know that's not the proper approach, and it would add a lot of overhead to what should be, otherwise, a very simple test. What do you do? Do you assume there is a reason you're not seeing for this solution? Do you respectfully disagree and bring up your point? Correcting your leader is never easy, but sometimes it needs to happen.

The leader is generally not the best developer on the team. This is a common misconception about leaders, mainly because senior developers are often promoted to team leads or managers, and they take that technical baggage with them. However, over time they start seeing a disconnect between their skills and those of the market. While they may try to keep up to date, they will never maintain the level of understanding that you, as a developer, can have. Any good leader should keep that in mind and control their ego when they're corrected by a developer in their team.

This is all to say, yes, you can correct your leader. Just be mindful of how you do it. While, in theory, egos should not play a part, not everyone can keep theirs under control all the time. If you find a problem with your lead's proposal, try to speak with them privately and highlight the issue.

A good way to bring this point up is to phrase it as a question, or as a potential learning experience for you. You've seen their proposal, and according to your understanding there is something missing, but maybe you're the one missing something. That way they won't feel like they're being attacked by you. This is crucial when trying to correct someone else, especially if that someone is hierarchically higher than you.

Great leads will not only welcome these instances, but they will also try to promote them within their team. They are completely aware that they're not the most technically sound member of their team and that the team itself will have a lot to add when it comes to making technical decisions and proposals.

The worst thing that can happen to a leader (whether because of their team or through their own fault) is that their team members don't feel like they can interject and correct them. That leaves the leader alone and potentially incorrectly assuming their team is always in agreement with them. So speak up and give your opinion. Don't be afraid to challenge your lead's ideas, but also be open to being corrected and educated by them as a response.

8.4 Dealing with clients

If you're working as a freelancer or as part of a consulting company, you'll have to deal with something that product company developers don't have to worry about: the client. The client is whoever is paying for the project you're working on, and because of that, they tend to believe they can meddle in the project's progress and even demand things that were never in scope. Of course, not every client is evil, and some of them understand that developing software is not a trivial task. However, those are not the norm—at least, that hasn't been my experience.

Dealing with clients is generally the task of your leader, and usually they will tackle that task while you focus on your job: moving the project forward. But what can you do if, during a demo call to show the client the latest set of features, the client starts complaining about missing features or unmet expectations? Should you say anything at all?

8.4.1 Correcting the client

You've probably heard the phrase "The customer is always right." I like to append to it, "until they're not." The fact of the matter is that the client is not always right. They're quite often wrong, but since they're the ones spending their money on the project, they think they're entitled to ask for anything and require crazy features. Those requests, if kept unchecked, can affect the progress of the project. The project lead, and sometimes even the developers, will have to correct the client when it comes to the project itself and the assumptions around it.

The main thing to understand is that while the client is the expert on their business, you and your teammates are the experts when it comes to developing a piece of software. This implies that you should not be trying to correct your client when they're stating facts or even assumptions about their business. That's their area of expertise, and if they say they'll be able to make it rain Coca Cola, you better believe them. However, the moment they start making assumptions about your side of the equation, such as assuming the difficulty of some tasks, roughly estimating others, or even suggesting changes mid-development, that's where you and your leader are completely entitled to say "No, you're wrong." Maybe not with those words, but you get the point. You have everything you need to justify your response, so make sure you use it.

Be careful with your "no"—as developers we tend to blurt out that word more often than we should. Anything that breaks our plans or implies more work than estimated is an immediate "no" for us. But if you're given the opportunity to be client-facing, it means your lead trusts you and your communication skills. This is major, so make sure you add the expected value.

If you have to correct the client, be considerate; try to have them explain their assumptions to the point where you can easily identify the problem in their reasoning and highlight it. But don't just say "That's the problem, that assumption is wrong." Try to explain why it's "not accurate" (notice how I'm no longer saying "wrong") and the impact that assumption will have on the project. Depending on the methodology you're working under (be it waterfall-like or agile), your team leads will either try to push back on those changes and additions or they'll welcome them as long as the plan can be adjusted. If they go with the latter, remember that more work should always equal more time (or rather, an update on the end date of the project). If it doesn't, you should raise your hand right away and say something (in private to your lead, not in front of the client). Change is not intrinsically wrong, and if it's handled properly, it should not generate problems, so don't say "no" right away.

Some words are too strong to be used in delicate conversations, such as with a client or potential client. Table 8.1 lists some of the most common ones to avoid.

Table 8.1   What not to say to your client

Forbidden phrase	Replacement phrase	Explanation
No.	Not exactly; we can think about that; what about doing X instead?	Soften the impact of "no," which can be considered a hard wall your client is hitting. Instead, gain some time, provide an alternative, or even highlight the downside of the client's proposal. If you can and are sure about it, provide a valid alternative as part of the conversation.
That's wrong.	That's not entirely accurate.	The word "wrong" can be taken personally, and it's absolute. Instead, reference the accuracy of the statement, implying that not everything is wrong about it—only a part of it is.
We have a problem.	We're facing a challenge/opportunity.	Problems worry paying clients. Instead, turn them into a challenge to improve your team and your project, or even into an opportunity to do something new.
Let me look into it.	I'll do some research and get back to you.	Don't be vague. Instead, show that you have an action already in mind and that you know what to do once you've found an answer.
I can't do anything about it.	I understand your frustration. I'll do some more research and get back to you.	There is always something you can do or suggest. You're here to help, so show you're doing everything you can.
Did you understand?	Am I explaining myself well?	Do not put the burden of miscommunication on your client (even when it is their fault). If you're trying to explain something to them, assume it's you who's not able to explain it correctly. Otherwise, they'll feel like you're treating them as stupid.

What happens, though, when you're doing everything right on your side, but the client is still mad or unhappy about the team's progress? Whose fault is that?

8.4.2 Angry clients

You might be doing everything right, and you might be using the right words, but the client can still be unhappy. And it's not your fault!

There are many moving parts in a software project, other than coding, of course. The original conversations between your company and the client are usually done by commercial people who do not necessarily take technology into consideration. And even when they do, those who estimate the effort may do so with very little information and base their estimates on assumptions that fall apart once the project starts.

I once worked for a client in the pharma industry who bought a project from my company, but they had been promised a lot of big results early on. We started working on the project without that understanding, and by the time we started delivering results, they were not what the client expected. The problem here was a failure to manage the client's expectations. We were doing everything we could to provide a great service, but the expectations were so high that nothing we did met them.

In the end, we finished the project and the client refused to pay. The problem went on to be handled by the legal departments of both companies, and they eventually settled on an agreement. Was it our fault? Not in the slightest, and I can say that because even though the circumstances weren't ideal, we tried to reset the expectations many times.

Don't get me wrong though. I'm not saying that every time a client dislikes your project, there is a reason that doesn't include you. Chances are that most of the time it's going to be your fault, and you'll have to accept it and find the best way to solve the problem.

But when the problem comes from another source, you can't just sit back and accept the circumstances. You still have to find a solution. If you do find one and solve your client's problems, you've not only managed to fix your project, but you've also gained your client's respect and admiration. It's not easy, and it's not always possible, but given the reward, it's definitely a worthy endeavor.

The key to a healthy client relationship is feedback. They need to be able to provide it in a safe environment, and you should know how to receive it. But that's not the only situation where feedback is important; internal feedback is just as relevant, so let's take a look at that.

8.5 Feedback is mandatory

Tell me if you've heard this before: you joined a new team about three months ago and you've been working daily, giving your best, and haven't run into any problems so far. Does that mean you're doing okay? Is everyone happy with your work? Or are they secretly expecting you to realize that you're making mistakes and fix them on your own? How can you tell? You can't. Not unless someone gives you feedback.

And guess what? The same applies to your leader. Some organizations don't really promote this practice, while others make it mandatory, but leaders should receive feedback from their teams. There is no objective way for them to understand if they're doing a good job or not, so let's close this chapter, and this book, with a primer on feedback.

8.5.1 Why is feedback so important?

Feedback is part of our everyday life. There is even a law of physics that covers feedback: "For every action there is an equal and opposite reaction." Granted, that's Newton's third law of motion, but it still covers feedback—in layman's terms, it's telling us that for everything we do, there is something telling us we did it. When it comes to our job, we sometimes forget about feedback and not only don't provide it when needed, but we also forget to request it.

Without feedback, we can only assume how well we're doing, and you know what I think about assumptions, so let's not do it like that. Your leader should provide feedback on a regular basis—that's part of what being a leader is.

If you're not getting that feedback, and it's been a while since you started working (a few months can be considered "a while"), you need to request it yourself. Notice how I say "need" and not "can." Feedback is one of the only tools at your disposal to understand whether you're doing a great job or if you need to adjust or improve in an area. Feedback is important to your career development, so it's your right as an employee to receive it and your duty to request it if it's not provided. Don't forget that.

As a team member, you should also be empowered to provide feedback, both to your leader and your teammates. Granted, part of that feedback could be anonymous, simplifying the task and giving those scared of speaking up the safety net they need to do it.

As a leader, feedback from your team can help you adapt your leading strategy if people say you're too hard on them, or perhaps you will change the way you assign tasks or handle meetings. There are many examples of areas where leaders can improve or change based on the opinion of their team.

As a team member, you can also use your leader's feedback to try to be more autonomous or perhaps more proactive when it comes to proposing new ideas. Perhaps you're not paying enough attention to your professional growth, or maybe you've used one of the phrases I mentioned in chapter 7 that should never be said to your manager. There are virtually infinite possibilities when it comes to feedback and places to improve, but these are the most common categories:

- *Autonomy*—Leaders always encourage you develop autonomy when it comes to deciding how to implement a task or how to solve a problem. The more autonomous the developer they're leading, the more time they'll have to handle everything else.
- *Consistency*—It's not enough to have a great month, or a great sprint (if you're working under scrum). You have to take what you did so well and replicate it every day. Make sure you ask for confirmation regarding what exactly made it such a great period, and try to work on doing it more.

- *Confidence in your work*—This one probably results from the previous two, but if you're autonomous enough to work by yourself and you still need validation from others, you're not making the most of the time you have. Instead, with time and through feedback, you should start trusting your skills more.
- *Soft skills*—These are important for every developer throughout their career. They won't be requested or treated as mandatory for junior developers, but the higher you go up the ladder, the more relevant they'll become. If you're just getting started, this is something to keep in mind, but nothing to worry about right now.

So, yes, feedback is important. But what exactly is feedback, and how many different ways can you provide this feedback? Let's analyze that.

8.5.2 Different types of feedback

If you don't overthink it, feedback is feedback. Someone is telling you what they think about you and your work. So why am I making such a big fuss about it? That's because I've worked for multiple companies that have handled feedback differently, and I've come to see slight differences that can actually make an impact.

The difference is in the formality and the target audience. Let's go over some common types of feedback:

- *Informal peer-to-peer feedback (microfeedback)*—This is the type of feedback you give your colleagues or they give you. It can happen at any given time, and it's usually focused on one particular action or interaction between the two of you. For example, maybe you helped them with a problem they were having, so they'll give you positive feedback about your willingness to help others.
- *Informal feedback from your leader*—This is the same as the previous point but coming from your leader. Usually it relates to outstanding behavior on your part and your leader wanting to recognize this. For instance, maybe you finished all your tasks two days early, or perhaps you highlighted a design problem with the current architecture.
- *Formal feedback from your leader*—This is more structured feedback relating to the company's cultural and technological priorities and giving you an idea of how well you fit within those standards. This is the type of feedback that is used by HR and other managers to determine if you deserve a raise or promotion.
- *Formal and anonymous feedback from the team*—Leaders should be constantly evaluated by the team they lead. Anonymous feedback is the perfect way to keep them accountable. If they're being too hard on their team or poorly managing their project, they should be hearing about it.

Your company might implement some or all of these, or maybe even other types of feedback I haven't mentioned. The point is that some form of feedback needs to be implemented, and ideally it should go both ways (from top to bottom and from bottom to top).

Whether there is a formal process or no process at all, you as an employee and a team member have can ask for a feedback session from your leader. You *need* to ask for it once every few months to make sure you're still moving in the right direction.

When it comes to when feedback should be provided, that depends on the type of feedback session:

- *Microfeedback sessions*—This feedback, either from other teammates or your leader, can happen at any time. If you have something to say or highlight, you should do it right away—a session of 15 minutes should be more than enough. If you're giving negative feedback (in the sense of highlighting negative aspects of your colleague), you should also give them time to process and reply to your feedback.

    If you're on the receiving end of negative feedback, make sure you don't immediately deny it or try to explain why the other person got it all wrong. If they're telling you that you're doing something wrong, and you know you're not, that's still the image you're transmitting to everyone else. So even if you don't think you're guilty of those assertions, you still risk looking like it if you overreact. Take a deep breath, and try to ask questions to understand how the other person reached this conclusion and determine the source of the confusion. That way you can pinpoint the mistake and explain what really happened. That is the best way to react to negative feedback. Avoid a knee-jerk response that you'll regret later.

    If, by any chance, the feedback is valid, and you do have problems to solve, consider asking for advice from the person who's giving you the feedback. If they're highlighting something you need to work on, they probably have a good idea of what you should be doing instead. They won't give you the exact steps to solve the problem, but their advice should be good enough to steer you in the right direction.

- *Formal feedback*—I suggest formal feedback should happen twice or perhaps three times every year. Formal feedback takes a lot longer; it encompasses the last few months of work, so it needs to cover multiple aspects of your performance. If it's done too often, it will cover very little, and if the time between feedback sessions is too long, it will cover too much, and there might be too much feedback. Twice or three times a year is just about right.

Finally, when it comes to giving feedback, consider these points to make the most of the session:

- *Be on time*. This shows you care about the person you're meeting with, which is crucial, because you're trying to connect with them. The feedback you're giving is important for the other person, so showing up late sends the message that you don't really care about them.
- *Be direct*. When giving feedback, you need to be absolutely certain that the other person is getting the same message you're trying to convey. This is especially true

when the feedback you're trying to provide is negative—you need the other person to understand exactly what you're saying. If there is a misunderstanding, they might not be able to react properly or even adjust or correct what you need them to.

- *Remember that you're interacting with another person.* Be caring when providing feedback. Whether it's positive or negative, the feedback is meant to motivate them to improve further. Don't just approach it as a transaction where you say what you need to, and then you're out. Try to explain the reasoning behind the feedback and give examples of situations or actions that led to you having this impression of the other person. Most of all, give them a chance to reply and ask questions if they need to. Turn the session into a conversation between two colleagues. The point is to give them a safe space to explain themselves. You should be open to changing your mind as well. Be critical about the response you get and about the reasons why you gave the feedback in the first place. Don't be afraid to say "I'm sorry I misunderstood the situation" and adjust accordingly.

- *You're giving feedback, not advice.* Remember this one. You're telling others what you think about their work, not what they should do to improve it. Giving feedback is great, but unsolicited advice is terrible.

- *Your feedback should focus on the professional aspects of your teammate.* This one sounds obvious, but if their performance is affected by personal problems they may be having, the temptation to talk about them will be high. Don't go into that rabbit hole—you won't come out of it untouched. Feedback should stop at the line between professional and personal life. If they have problems outside of work, they need to work on them however they see fit. Do not meddle.

Feedback is paramount for everyone's career development, and you have to remember that you should be giving feedback to your leader as much as the company culture will let you. You also need to request feedback every few months to understand whether you're doing things right or if you need to adjust your course.

8.6 Thank you

You've reached the end of this chapter and, with it, the end of the book. Thank you for coming with me on this journey. For me it was a walk down memory lane, and I hope you've gained something by walking it with me: insights, lessons learned, or at least confirmation that you're not alone in this career you've started. If you're coming out of this book with any of those things, I'll consider this book a complete success.

The last thing to remember is that if you feel like you're going through this alone or you have no one to talk about it with, you can always reach out to me. I won't leave my contact details here because they change over time (some of them do, anyway), but you should be able to google my name and find me.

The last piece of knowledge and wisdom I'd like to leave you with is the answer to everything and every question you've ever had. Use it well: 42.

Thank you!

Summary

- Your leader is not out to get you. If they keep nagging you about a status update or the chances of your features being delayed, that's because they need to know in order to transmit that information to someone else.

- Even if you don't like the type of tasks being assigned, there is a good reason why your lead has given them to you. Don't reject the tasks; they may be given to you because they'll help you improve your skills, or because you're the best at doing them. Make the most of them.

- All projects are a lot more complex than they look from the outside. Even if you're coding within the project, you might still be missing the big picture. Be mindful about things such as scope creep, poorly handled assumptions, and parallel assignments that might affect your performance.

- Your leader is not always going to be right. They're there to help coordinate the team of experts, and as such, part of your obligation is to highlight any problems for them.

- Clients aren't always easy to deal with, and once you start getting client-facing time, you'll have to work on your soft skills to better communicate with them.

- Feedback should be mandatory, both for people leading teams, so they can stay accountable for their actions, and for team members, so they can understand if they're doing everything right or not. If you're not getting feedback every few months, consider requesting it from those directly working with you. Even if it's informal feedback and doesn't take into consideration things like promotions or a salary raise, you'll still learn a lot from it.

index

A new online reading experience

liveBook, our online reading platform, adds a new dimension to your Manning books, with features that make reading, learning, and sharing easier than ever. A liveBook version of your book is included FREE with every Manning book.

This next generation book platform is more than an online reader. It's packed with unique features to upgrade and enhance your learning experience.

- Add your own notes and bookmarks
- One-click code copy
- Learn from other readers in the discussion forum
- Audio recordings and interactive exercises
- Read all your purchased Manning content in any browser, anytime, anywhere

As an added bonus, you can search every Manning book and video in liveBook—even ones you don't yet own. Open any liveBook, and you'll be able to browse the content and read anything you like.*

Find out more at www.manning.com/livebook-program.

*Open reading is limited to 10 minutes per book daily